The System Has a Soul is a marvelous collection of
of subjects with which serious Christians must deal... ...
should be in every pastor's library.

FRANCIS J. BECKWITH
Professor of Philosophy & Church-State Studies
Baylor University

Hunter Baker is one of the stars of the rising generation of Christian public intellectuals. The hallmark of his work is a combination of analytical rigor, moral seriousness, and lucid writing. He engages secular traditions of thought critically but
respectfully, paying points of view he does not himself share the compliment of
understanding them thoughtfully and presenting them accurately. He is a thinker,
not a mere rhetorician. He keeps his eye on the prize, namely, getting to the truth
of the matter.

ROBERT P. GEORGE
McCormick Professor of Jurisprudence
Princeton University

Hunter Baker has once again produced a most engaging and masterfully written
volume on a smorgasbord of subjects, including discussions of church and state,
faith and culture, education and economics, secularism and society, as well as
religion and politics. *The System Has a Soul* builds on Baker's previous outstanding
works and offers a veritable feast for the readers of this volume. Readers looking
for more than a descriptive survey of these important subjects will be pleased with
the substantive interaction as well as the thoughtful and constructive proposals that
Baker provides. I gladly recommend this volume.

DAVID S. DOCKERY
President
Trinity International University

These essays represent a deep engagement with the challenges of a secularizing
culture from the perspective of confessional Christianity. Anyone seeking to relate
the gospel to the culture (and that should be all of us) will benefit from this wisdom.

RUSSELL D. MOORE
President
Southern Baptist Ethics & Religious Liberty Commission

THE SYSTEM HAS A SOUL

THE SYSTEM HAS A SOUL

ESSAYS ON CHRISTIANITY, LIBERTY, AND POLITICAL LIFE

HUNTER BAKER

GRAND RAPIDS · MICHIGAN

The System Has a Soul: Essays on Christianity, Liberty, and Political Life

Cover image: Looking up at Trinity Church in downtown Manhattan
Author: Greg Goodman
Source: http://www.adventuresofagoodman.com
Photo is used with permission.

Scripture taken from the New American Standard Bible®, Copyright © 1960, 1962, 1963, 1968, 1971, 1972, 1973, 1975, 1977, 1995 by The Lockman Foundation. Used by permission.

ISBN: 978-193894894-7

Library of Congress Cataloging-in-Publication Data

Baker, Hunter, 1970–
    The system has a soul : essays on Christianity, liberty, and political life /
    Hunter Baker

CHRISTIAN'S LIBRARY PRESS
    An imprint of the Acton Institute
    for the Study of Religion & Liberty
98 E. Fulton
Grand Rapids, Michigan 49503
Phone: 616.454.3080
Fax: 616.454.9454
www.clpress.com

Cover design by Peter Ho
Interior composition by Judy Schafer

Printed in the United States of America

This book is dedicated to Robert Sloan.
He was my friend and mentor
at just the right time.

CONTENTS

ACKNOWLEDGMENTS

T he essays in this volume are the fruit of a particularly good run of opportunities offered to me to write and speak after the publication of my first book, *The End of Secularism*. I thank Crossway for publishing that volume and my second book, *Political Thought: A Student's Guide*. The Acton Institute offered me the chance to put these essays and addresses together in this collection. I am grateful to them. Acton has been both an inspiration to me and a partner.

Some of the works you see here originally appeared in *Touchstone: A Journal of Mere Christianity*. Specifically, the reflections on my grandfather's time in the US Postal Service, Christian schools and race, and the French and American revolutions all first appeared in similar form in that journal. Two essays, one on secularism as a form of social leveling and another on common ground for libertarians and conservatives, were published in *Religion & Liberty*. The essay on secularism as social leveling had its genesis in endowed lectures given at Southern Seminary, which had the same title as this book. The essay has also since been translated and published in a Polish-language journal. Acton's *Journal of Markets & Morality* first published my long talk on social justice, government, and society, which was originally given as the Calihan Lecture on the occasion of receiving the Novak Award in 2011. Some of the argumentation in this essay also appeared in *Political Thought: A Student's Guide.* The essay recounting the many difficulties with secularism was first presented at Hillsdale College as part of one of their Center for Constructive Alternatives events. The essay on secular statism and the problems it poses for religious liberty originally took the form of an address given at a Catholic church in Tennessee for the Fortnight of Freedom.

I offer my thanks to all of these partners for helping me to put ideas into the arena and for their important work. Thanks also to the institutions that have been meaningful to me in my career. These include The Rutherford Institute, Prison Fellowship, Georgia Family Council (now the Georgia Center for Opportunity), Baylor University, Houston Baptist University, and Union University.

INTRODUCTION

F or several years, I have been speaking and writing about the connections between religion, politics, and culture. When I first began thinking about politics, it was in the context of the Cold War. My generation is probably the last one to experience that conflict in such a way as to really remember it.

Throughout my first two decades of life, the two powers of the Cold War—the United States and the Soviet Union—appeared to be permanently camped on the precipice of all-out nuclear war. The phrase "mutually assured destruction" was actually somewhat reassuring because it seemed to point to some kind of ultimate brake. Nevertheless, I went to bed virtually every night of my teenage existence praying to God that he would not allow nuclear war to occur. I wanted to live a full life, get married, have children, and have a career. I had many conversations with peers about what we would do if a nuclear missile were on its way. The options seemed to be to go toward the bomb or run away from the bomb. Neither was obviously any good.

Until essentially the beginning of the end of the Cold War, I was not a Christian. I was more of a typical American youth. My religious faith was largely confined to asking God for things that I wanted. He was a genie to me. Other than that, I did not think about him very often. I was a political conservative for two reasons. The first was that my parents leaned that way. The second was Ronald Reagan. Like many young people in my generation, I found him to be a reassuring presence as a leader when Jimmy Carter had not seemed so.

It would not be until I went to college at Florida State University that I would experience a conversion to the Christian faith. At that time I began to perceive more dimensions to the Cold War than I had observed before. It was about more than just a free economy versus a planned and centrally directed one. The truth of the matter is that the fundamental cleavage between the Soviets and the Americans was largely spiritual in nature. Whittaker Chambers' accurate perception of that fact is responsible for the powerful impact of his book *Witness*. What is man? Is there a God? Do human beings have significance at the individual level? How important is freedom? Is religion a mere opiate designed to control the masses, or does it have some much greater significance? What kinds of actions can be justified in the course of trying to create a purportedly perfect society? What did it mean that Chambers could discern marvelous design in the intricacies of his child's ear?

One of the most powerful lessons that can be drawn from Chambers' story has to do with Christian anthropology and what that means for utopian plans and their implementation. In 1981, Warren Beatty produced and directed a film titled *Reds* about the Communist revolution in Russia and its impact on fellow travelers in the United States. Beatty played American John Reed, the author of *Ten Days That Shook the World*, and an enthusiast for the action of the masses against the capitalists, whom he believed were exploiting them. Though the portrayal of the revolution is largely sympathetic, it is clear that the stumbling blocks of the revolution have to do with the revolutionaries themselves.

There is a scene in the film that captures in a nutshell this concern about the nature of man and the other matters discussed in the essays that follow. In Russia, John Reed meets with fellow revolutionary Emma Goldman. The revolution has settled into an ugly aftermath manifesting conflict, terror, and repression in the wake of the initial euphoria. Goldman expresses her great disappointment with the progress to date. The people are not in power. Dissent is punished with execution. The government's most potent weapons are fear and intimidation. Indeed, millions have been killed, and these deaths occurred *after* Russia exited World War I. For these reasons, she wants out. The revolution has not made life better. And the supposed brotherhood of the workers has not resulted in peace but in continuing violent conflict. Rather than being more free, people are less free.

Reed, at least at this point, has not been affected in the same way Goldman has. Does she not realize that the revolution has enemies trying to undermine it? Did she think that the revolution would be able to go forward without using the methods of war and terror? These things will be necessary in order to achieve the greater good of the revolution's goals. Human beings will never throw off their shackles unless there are men who have the stomach to do what is necessary. Goldman is taken aback. As committed as she has been to the struggle, she did not foresee the rotten fruit that would form on the vine.

Reed, despite his proper revolutionary spirit in that moment, becomes increasingly disillusioned and ultimately ends up arguing with Russian comrades in the elite class (even the most egalitarian revolutions have them) that the heart of revolution is dissent and that the individual matters. His voice is faltering with his health. He dies confused and wrung out like an ill-used dishrag.

In that scene, I detect a number of the themes that have motivated me to think, write, and speak. But the core of it is something like this: I agree with those who have argued that original sin is the only empirically proven religious doctrine. Man is fallen. And no matter how much we might like to put our hopes on some king or purportedly clear-eyed secular prophet, we are bound to learn the lesson of ancient Israel that there really is no man fit to rule, not in the long run anyway. There is only one king, who is God. We must not seek to immanentize the eschaton (or bring forth the end of history). William F. Buckley Jr. and his young conservatives were right to say so. And life will not go any better (perhaps worse, if the twentieth century is any indication) if the work of making the world perfect through coercion is committed by the irreligious, secularists, or atheists, than if it were done by people moved by revelation.

Rather, I think we should accept the truth about ourselves and, thus, be skeptical about what good we might do with power. Christians should seek God's help in moving them further along the path of sanctification, but it is not a path along which anyone can really be forced. Someday every knee will bow and every tongue will confess, but that will not happen because we created the perfect political coalition or constructed an ingenious public policy. Christ the king will bend those knees and bring truth forth from those tongues by the majesty of his presence and the undeniability of his glory. Our task is to maintain the freedom of the church to continue to bear witness to those inside our nations and beyond. We must also fulfill the mission of the church to call men and women to govern themselves by submitting to God's rule in their lives, and to insist that the state do the good (and limited) work which God has entrusted to it, and that the state not engage in more grandiose works designed to take that which belongs ultimately to God more than it does to Caesar.

One

REFLECTIONS ON SOCIAL JUSTICE, GOVERNMENT, AND SOCIETY

The term *social justice* has been prominent in the evangelical world of late, especially among young people. Social justice was a major theme President Obama used to reach out to disaffected evangelicals and evangelical young people who felt excessively cabined in by a combination of conservative philosophies and triumphal patriotism that they believed was contrary to the gospel and their own sense of the good. The social justice message has offered an appealing way for the modern Left to supplement the thinness of a thoroughgoing secularism and scientism with a quasi-religious call for economic solidarity. Where the Left may be absent on bioethics, it can be present in economics.

We have heard this intriguing term invoked more frequently in the past several years. The call is not for justice, but for something more specific called social justice. What is it? How should we view it? What should we do about it?

The primary concern of social justice does not resemble the justice a family member demands when someone has been hurt, killed, or otherwise victimized. Social justice appears to be mostly about distributive concerns. Who is getting what in a given society? Just to ask that question seems to presume that some entity should have power to distribute or redistribute resources. Another way of looking at social justice is to examine whether social arrangements benefit the people of a political community. Do the laws and social understandings broadly benefit everyone or do they only work well for the wealthy and powerful?

Although the phrase *social justice* has just recently come back into vogue, both the words and the fundamental concern have long been common preoccupations of the critics of capitalism. I would like to begin by reviewing the basic case against a free economy and then questioning that case. I will then move on to propose what I think is a better way forward.

Critics of the Free Economy

One of the major arguments advanced by critics of the free economy has been that it only works to enrich wealthy owners while making everyone else either worse off or no better off. Karl Marx is probably the most influential person to make that argument. In his 1848 *Communist Manifesto*, Marx (along with Engels) pointed to the negative effects of industrial capitalism on the nature of work (reducing it to deadening simplicity and repetition), the distinctiveness of cultures (pushing them aside in favor of commodities), and vastly increasing inequality (as great fortunes became possible). Though he was moderately pleased that capitalism was sweeping away the old European order, he viewed it as a fatally flawed system that simply could not survive its own massive liabilities.[1]

Thorstein Veblen's *The Theory of the Leisure Class* criticized capitalism as a social trap maintained by the wealthy to ensure their position at the top. By keeping everyone focused on the need to conspicuously consume commercial goods as a way to demonstrate social status, the rich had effectively placed the masses on a giant hamster wheel designed to keep them working and consuming, thus missing opportunities for leisure and development of higher goals. Whatever gains could be claimed for industrial efficiency are eaten

---

1. The 1848 manifesto is widely available in the common domain. It may be accessed online at http://www.gutenberg.org/ebooks/61.

up by senseless consumption created by social manipulation of the people.[2]

Veblen also suggested that advances in mechanization (a feature of the free and innovative economy) had not actually made the lives of workers any easier. They worked as hard as ever (or harder) without any corresponding improvement in their quality of life. All of this proceeded from the fact of private ownership, which Veblen viewed as an artifact of the more predatory forms of culture that preceded our own.

In 1906, Upton Sinclair published his treatment of life in and around the slaughterhouses of Chicago, *The Jungle*. The book is still widely read today. He contrasted the good quality of life in simple, rural existence with the brutality of making a living in the unclean, unsafe, frozen commercial nightmare of the Chicago slaughterhouses. He succeeded in drawing great attention to questions of food purity, worker safety, and the potential harshness of capitalism. The workers in his story often had to pay kickbacks to get a job, risk their lives and health to earn their paychecks, and then fend off a small army of swindlers and con men in order to save anything for their families.[3]

Writing only a dozen years later, Walter Rauschenbusch produced *Christianizing the Social Order*. He argued that business and capitalism represented the unregenerate portion of the social order. In one especially memorable segment, he claimed that if business were a foreign island, we would send missionaries to it! While he conceded that the competitive features of capitalism had perhaps been useful in order to help create economic prosperity, he contended that the time for competition had passed. In his eyes, competition was the commercial version of warfare. And who wanted to be at war? In addition, unregenerate capitalism made possible all kinds of fraud and thievery. The villain "from his office chair" can "pick a thousand pockets, poison a thousand sick, pollute a thousand minds."[4]

---

2. Thorstein Veblen, *The Theory of the Leisure Class* (New York: Macmillan, 1899).

3. Upton Sinclair, *The Jungle* (New York: Doubleday, 1906).

4. Walter Rauschenbusch, *Christianizing the Social Order* (New York: Macmillan, 1912). With regard to the specific quote, it appears Rauschenbusch was echoing sentiments expressed (essentially word for word) earlier by

We can follow Rauschenbusch with John Dewey, the Midwestern professor who exerted a gigantic influence on American culture, most specifically in education. Dewey's 1935 *Liberalism and Social Action* repeated some of the themes reviewed so far. Our science and production have taken great leaps forward, but the lives of human beings have not. Private ownership has prevented the benefits of advances from being broadly distributed. Competition may have had its uses in the overall evolution of human economic effort, but it is no longer valid. To these themes he added the suggestion that politics should be under scientific control. Under that scientific control, the forces of production could be socialized for maximum benefit. Although he rejected Marx's idea of violent revolution as a mere dogma, Dewey reserved the right to employ violence against a recalcitrant minority.[5] In the middle of the Great Depression with doubts about the free economy apparently reinforced by empirical reality, Dewey's proposal did not necessarily appear extreme.

Fast-forward about three decades to John Kenneth Galbraith's *The Affluent Society*. The book was originally published at the end of the 1950s. Galbraith surveyed history since the beginning of the development of the central tradition of economic thought. He saw a social science steeped in pessimistic thinking and nearly obsessed with the matter of scarcity. Galbraith was convinced that this focus on scarcity was a reasonable conclusion of the early economists because of the dominant impact of need and want on human beings throughout most of their recorded existence. In Galbraith's account, these men thought that even if better methods of production were to increase wealth, that wealth would be eaten up by human beings having more babies and having to provide for them. Thus, men would never rise much above laboring for simple subsistence.[6]

Eager to displace what he called "the conventional wisdom" (Galbraith may have actually coined that term) with a new way of thinking, the Harvard economist pointed to a phenomenon early econ-

---

Edward A. Ross in *Sin and Society: An Analysis of Latter-Day Iniquity* (Boston: Houghton-Mifflin, 1907).

5. John Dewey, *Liberalism and Social Action* (New York: G. P. Putnam, 1935).

6. John Kenneth Galbraith, *The Affluent Society: 40th Anniversary Edition* (New York: Mariner Books, 1998), 23.

omists could not have predicted and did not factor into their thinking. What was it? Standing in America just shy of 1960, Galbraith noted that human beings in the West had experienced "a mountainous rise in well-being." Dwell on that momentarily. "A mountainous rise in well-being."[7] This great change is evidenced by the existence of "The Affluent Society," in which we no longer need to order our affairs around the notion of scarcity.

Interestingly, Galbraith did not spend much time reflecting on the *cause* of that mountainous rise, though the most likely answer would be something like democratic capitalism. For a man dedicated to debunking the conventional wisdom through clarity of analysis, the omission appears strange. As I examined his argument, I kept wondering how he could make so little of the fact that this new state of affairs—increased real wages, increased opportunity, increased production, better material living conditions, a quantum leap above what human beings experienced just a century or so earlier—coincided with the rise of a modern, free-market economy and the innovation unleashed by it. Or rather, perhaps he chose not to spend any time extolling the value of competitive capitalism because he likely viewed it the same way Rauschenbusch and Dewey did, which is to say that it was something like a necessary state in our social evolution but one that is better left behind.

The big point that should not be missed here is that Galbraith implicitly conceded that earlier critics of the free economy had been wrong in their repeated assertions that competitive capitalism failed to yield broad benefits to the public. It was obvious that it did yield those benefits in the form of (let me say it once more in Galbraith's words) "a mountainous rise in well-being." If Galbraith was right to observe (if rather obliquely) that capitalism has been the system in place during a period of phenomenal growth in prosperity for human beings generally, then the primary argument of competitive capitalism's critics is void. The free market does result in broad distribution of benefits from economic activity. For a modern demonstration of that to which Galbraith merely alluded, one could look to the recent Heritage Foundation report on poverty in America that illustrates

---

7. Galbraith, *The Affluent Society*, 65.

the astounding degree to which even those officially classified as "poor" enjoy the results of economic advance.[8]

Evidence of this kind has not gone unnoticed though it may sometimes seem to be the case. The celebrated sociologist Peter Berger wrote in his recent intellectual autobiography that he started out more or less agnostic between socialism and capitalism, but ultimately came down squarely on the capitalist side:

> Capitalism has lifted millions of people from dehumanizing misery to a decent standard of living. In other words, the myth of growth holds out a promise that, by and large, is empirically valid. By contrast, no socialist revolution has ever fulfilled its promise, not even in cases that were more humane than that of the Chinese Communists.[9]

The central critique of capitalism has been that it fails to provide broad-based benefits. It is also clearly untrue.

Of course, as the empirical situation has changed, so has the argument. Critics of the free market now argue more on the basis of inequality and relative deprivation instead of on the basis of absolute deprivation. This point is harder to dispute. There is little doubt that economic freedom will lead to stratification in terms of wealth and income. We should not fail to notice here, though, that relative deprivation is a very different thing from absolute deprivation. The moral force of it is not nearly so strong. If one neighbor is able to purchase a new BMW and the man next door can only afford a used Chevrolet, it is a very different situation than if one man sits upon a pile of ready cash while his neighbor starves. Add the possibility that the same system that allows for relative deprivation may well result in a higher general standard of living for all (yielding such advances as antibiotics, air-conditioning, and cell phones) and the moral force of pointing to its existence is even less compelling.

---

8. Robert Rector and Rachel Sheffield, "Understanding Poverty in the United States: Surprising Facts about America's Poor," posted on September 13, 2011. The Heritage Foundation report may be accessed at http://www.heritage.org/research/reports/2011/09/understanding-poverty-in-the-united-states-surprising-facts-about-americas-poor.

9. Peter Berger, *Adventures of an Accidental Sociologist: How to Explain the World without Becoming a Bore* (New York: Prometheus Books, 2011), 131.

It should also be noted, as Thomas Sowell has often written, that a free economy is a dynamic economy. Winners are not always winners and many different people occupy varied positions on the ladder of success at points in their lives.[10] The indictment against inequality is not so strong if mobility along the scale is possible. How many of us can point to arcs of mobility within our families as generations have moved from subsistence family farms to blue collar work to professional work, advanced degrees, or entrepreneurial opportunities? Clearly, the system has not been a static one such as the rigid and paternalistic chain that existed in old Europe and was so well described with mixed emotions by Alexis de Tocqueville in his work on America.

Another important point is that even if we drag everyone back to the starting line, those with talent and drive will again move to the head of the pack. In his classic case against government efforts to bring about equality, Robert Nozick observed that the only way to ensure equality is continuous interference by the government.[11] That continuous interference should be seen as a major threat to human freedom.

There are negative practical consequences, as well. What tends to happen is that if the government changes the basis of economic advance, say from economic achievement to some ideological goal such as equality, then those who are able to cultivate political networks are likely to enjoy the highest standards of living. One might ask which system of reward is likely to provide more innovation and efficiency to the benefit of the broader society: one that rewards skill, work, and expertise or one that rewards political acumen? It is possible to have an equality-based society that produces more even economic shares, *nearly all of which are smaller* than most of the unequal shares in a free economy.

But what about another major charge lodged against competitive capitalism, which is that it leads to fraud, theft, and negligence from unscrupulous operators? The first answer is that such things

---

10. For an example, see Thomas Sowell, *The Vision of the Anointed: Self-Congratulation as a Basis for Public Policy* (New York: Basic Books, 1995), 48–49.

11. Robert Nozick, *Anarchy, State, and Utopia* (New York: Basic Books, 2013), 163.

clearly exist in a free economy. Upton Sinclair's *The Jungle* aptly demonstrated the potential ills of a production economy run for short-term gain to the exclusion of all other considerations. We could point to Enron as an example of the sorts of fraud that can emerge in a modern corporation. Players all along the spectrum in a free economy can be cheats or frauds.

An immediate answer to the problem is that the existence of competition can remedy the existence of shady operators. People will not long do business with someone who is defrauding them. We hear Sinclair's story and push for more federal regulation, but his exposé would also have created opportunities for competitors willing to make guarantees of better safety and cleanliness in their production. The Enrons eventually are exposed and lose their market share.

Nevertheless, with freedom comes the possibility of gain from unethical behavior. That objection is undoubtedly true. There is little question that these bad acts have happened, are happening, and will happen. The first answer is that competition allows for fairly rapid natural reform because bad actors cannot hold their customer base. But the second answer comes in the form of a question: If human beings can create negative outcomes through their bad acts in a free society, how much worse and how much more comprehensive can the possible effects be when the acts of individuals or groups are wedded to extensive government power?

The critics of competition deplore what they perceive as the great waste of effort caused by human beings trying to excel one another in the market. Cooperation, in their minds, is the answer. The problem with cooperation is that *cooperation for* can just as easily become *cooperation against*. Governments with the loftiest goals have often become the enemies of their people. And power, once centralized with a noble purpose, is extraordinarily difficult to limit and disperse. Competition may not be optimal in the same way democracy probably underperforms government by a saintly king, but it is a decidedly lower risk proposition in a fallen world.

Social Justice and the Role of the Government

Thus far, I have addressed some of the criticisms lodged against capitalism by partisans of a particular type of social justice that is sympathetic to the use of greater government power to bring about a closer approximation of a kind of equality believed to be more just. Rather than simply defending capitalism or the free market against the arguments against them, I want to spend some time addressing a major structural problem I perceive in the call for social justice in which social justice implies redistribution and strong government efforts to create equal conditions rather than equality before the law. My question is this: Is government the right instrument for achieving the kinds of gains enthusiasts of social justice want to accomplish? Is there something in the nature of the achievement of that goal, especially in terms of constant interference and coercion of those who have not committed wrongs, which should lead us to look for a different solution?

Should there be a connection between government and justice? Undoubtedly. But we have to find the right connection. What does it look like for government to properly dispense its function of providing justice?

Stanley Fish once highlighted the reason for his antifoundational stance on morality by pointing to the very different positions people take on fairness.[12] He is right to a point. While one man might think fairness is vindicated through the enforcement of a formal set of rules, another might think fairness requires much more, such as active intervention, compensation for differences, redistribution, and so on. So, yes, people have different positions. But we would be remiss if we failed to notice that there is a common denominator. The second man would not want to do away with the formal rules. For example, the common rule of the classroom is that professors assign grades on the basis of performance. If the professor were to hand out grades in a random distribution, virtually everyone would be outraged. But let us imagine a professor who decides to redistribute points from more successful students to other students he perceives to have a social claim of some kind to grade assistance. There would likely be a significant disagreement between students as to whether the practice is justified. The difference over the much disputed social redistribution of points over against the near unanimity of the com-

---

12. Stanley Fish, "Mission Impossible: Settling the Just Bounds between Church and State," *Columbia Law Review* 97 (December 1997): 2255–2333.

mon rule that professors give students the grade they earn rather than random marks helps highlight the degree to which governments can or should attempt to provide justice.

Government will be most successful, Milton Friedman contended, when it acts as an umpire or referee enforcing the formal procedural rules of the game. When it begins to attempt to affect substantive outcomes through active interference, it sets citizens against each other and threatens the social cohesion necessary for the broader society.[13]

The formal rules that government should make and enforce can be found in the fundamental purposes of law. None of us are free if we do not have basic justice and order. Martin Luther wrote in *On Secular Authority* that men and women need a lawful order in the same way they need food, air, and water.[14] When we read news accounts about people living in zones of extreme oppression and lawlessness such as have existed in Sudan due to ethnic hatreds or in Mexico because of drug cartels, we realize that the innocent men and women living in those places are unable to do much more than survive. They cannot build any kind of a life because whatever they do can be destroyed or stolen at any time. Surely, the most common denominator of our understanding of justice is the prevention of (and punishment of) the life-, property-, and freedom-destroying evil committed by those who do not recognize even the most basic duties of human beings toward each other. If government cannot put on a convincing show of accomplishing this goal, political scientists begin to employ the terminology "failed state."

Recognizing this reality, Luther construed the Sermon on the Mount to mean that the Christian must suffer any assault or insult to his person, but should always act to protect his neighbor. Government has been ordained in order to restrain predatory, evil people and to prevent them from victimizing everyone else. On that logic, a Christian could certainly serve under the government, and

---

13. Milton Friedman, *Capitalism and Freedom: 40th Anniversary Edition* (Chicago: University of Chicago Press, 2002), 23–24.

14. Martin Luther, "On Secular Authority," in *Luther and Calvin on Secular Authority*, ed. and trans. Harro Höpfl (Cambridge: Cambridge University Press, 1991), 13–14.

even take people's lives when acting with authority to protect the innocent.[15]

The implication here (and you could reason to this point using John Locke just as well as Luther) is that those who do wrong make themselves justly vulnerable to restraint, coercion, and correction by the state. If some people by their unrighteous acts have made themselves fit subjects for coercion and restraint, then what does that say about those who do not commit wrongs against others? The logical corollary is that those who do not commit wrongs should be free and uncoerced. They have earned the right to be free and uncoerced because they govern themselves. *In other words, if one does justice to others by not harming them through force or fraud, then one should be able to live free of government coercion and expect protection from wrongful coercion by others.*

One reader of this text asked me why I would start with those who do wrong and reason back to the freedom deserved by those who do not do wrong. The reason is that we more readily identify justice through its violation and remedy than we do through positive visions. We know when we have suffered an injustice that requires a remedy. We are far less certain about whether positive conditions of justice have been met. The common basis of justice is understood in its breach.

Order, justice, and freedom are clearly related. Justice is the result of the enforcement of a *moral* order that protects the freedom of human beings from malignant interference. We are able to live together in peace and freedom with the government standing by to exercise coercion and restraint upon those who would do wrong.

What about the word *equality*, one we also tend to associate with justice? The most realistic kind of equality we can achieve is an equality before the law. Every citizen should be able to expect the same treatment by the government: liberty and protection for the one who lives rightly, coercion and punishment for the one who does wrong.

Is equality before the law, freedom, and protection from those who would do evil justice enough? The persecuted women and children of Darfur would likely leap at the chance to make a life under such conditions. Men and women living in Mexico currently witness a

---

15. Luther, "On Secular Authority," 15.

deadly struggle between the forces of the legitimate government and the drug cartels, which are increasingly armed with sophisticated weapons and are trying to impose their ungodly order upon everyone. They yearn for their officials to enforce the peace. As these oppressed people hope for justice, they are looking for the government to perform its God-given function in restraining these evil men who willfully commit murder and foment mayhem in local communities. Justice will be done when the government puts down this malevolent rebellion against both earthly and heavenly kingdoms.

But there are others, envisioning something like a political analog for Maslow's famed hierarchy of needs, who would earnestly reject such a conception of justice as too limited. Equality before the law is not enough, they might say, because even that results in substantial inequalities in the experience of life. Some have billions of dollars, while others spend most of their lives paying off debts or, perhaps worse, are unable to even gain access to credit so as to run up debts. Some will travel the world, while others may never get far from the place of their birth. More prosaically, some will grow up in a home with two parents who love each other and provide a good example, guidance, support, and financial assistance, while others will have an unmarried mother and virtually no ready-made advantages to take into their development of a life and career.

What do those facts tell us about justice? Does the sheer fact of the difference in what some have and others do not justify government intervention to create balance? Once the scales are balanced, say, through substantial redistribution of wealth, how will stratifications be prevented from reemerging? And why do we focus mostly on difference manifested in terms of wealth? Some have better personalities and more rewarding friendships. Others have more natural strength or physical beauty. Some go through life with outstanding health and no allergies. We cannot redistribute these things unless we go the lengths of the absurdity envisioned by Kurt Vonnegut's story "Harrison Bergeron" in which the nation is ruled by a Handicapper General of the United States who finds ways to nullify *every* advantage. The Handicapper General is the absurd end of the trail of reasoning that demands continuous interference in the name of distributive (or redistributive) justice.[16]

Majoritarian tyranny (a strong word, but one naturally associated with the easy resort to coercion) was a prime concern of many American founders, which explains the many difficulties purposely built into our constitutional design intended to frustrate easy action. The great chronicler and observer of the young American nation, Alexis de Tocqueville, thought majoritarianism posed a threat potentially greater than that of an absolutist government because of the moral certitude crowds often associate with their numbers.[17] The point is straightforward. Majority decision making is highly logical as a matter of process, but the proper subjects of those decisions are not nearly so obvious. The action of a majority can be just or unjust. The example of modern day Greece is instructive. In 2011, nearly a third of the citizens had government jobs. Generous retirement packages became available at age sixty. Faced with news of the unsustainability of this state of affairs, citizens rioted. If it were possible to solve the problem by confiscating the wealth of citizens making more than a specified sum each year, one supposes a majority of voters would have jumped at the chance. Would they have been right to do so? Of course, no such magic was actually available. Mass confiscations have occurred in other times and places without solving problems. It was said of the Romans that at the end of the empire taxes were high and the coffers were empty.

No matter how much many Americans, and of late many young evangelicals, would like to think so, large transfers of wealth authorized by a majority of citizens do not create social justice. Rather, they raise serious questions about injustice. Many of those subject to the transfer will have done nothing to merit suffering a financial penalty in order to bring about better conditions for other citizens. They are not suitable subjects of coercion. Force is what lies behind the often friendly face of government action. It should be employed with great reluctance and only when all other solutions have been exhausted.

---

16. The futuristic short story has been much anthologized. My students report to me that it is still assigned in high schools.

17. Alexis de Tocqueville, *Democracy in America*, vol. 1, pt. 2, chap. 7.

Where I have left things so far will be a source of great frustration to many well-intentioned people. Michael Sandel, professor and teacher of the famous and popular "Justice" course at Harvard, would likely be one of them. He divides political thought into two primary camps. One is based on *the abstract, choosing self*, which guards freedom of decision and action fairly zealously against the notion of group-imposed duties. The other proceeds from *the situated self*, which fully accepts the great solidarity it should feel with other selves in a community and should easily accept nonconsensual duties that attach for no greater reason than that one is part of a particular group of people at a certain time. Community is like family in this account.[18] The situated self should feel a Bobby Kennedy–esque drive to use government to redistribute wealth for the good of the community.

Christians who push for social justice are, I think, motivated by this account of the situated self who sees himself or herself wedded in solidarity with the other members of the community and very much ready to put the government in service of this bond. The situated self does not see redistributive taxation and the social control of business as coercion so much as he or she sees virtue at work. For Christians, this view can be very attractive and it has proven so for young evangelicals especially.

If the situation were as Sandel presents it (basically an either/ or between a cold, impersonal freedom and a rich, warm-hearted nicely coercive government), then I would probably feel constrained to opt for the latter choice. But I believe that Sandel is committing an error by putting the burden of social solidarity on law and government. What if it is the case that government is potentially very good at providing the more limited type of peace, order, and justice to which I referred earlier, and is much less good at creating the conditions for some kind of idyllic vision of justice between persons that requires continuous government intervention and readjustment of circumstances? What if there were other strategies that could be placed in the service of civic affection and solidarity?

Peter Drucker once listened to John Kenneth Galbraith give a lecture in which he acted as if government and business were the only

---

18. Michael J. Sandel, *Justice: What's the Right Thing to Do?* (New York: Farrar, Strauss, and Giroux, 2010), 208–43.

two sectors in society. He spoke with him afterwards and reminded him that there was an entire sector left out of the discussion and that Galbraith's own Harvard University was part of that sector. Would it make more sense to look to government to remain within its core competency of administering the more fundamental form of justice and then embark upon a strategy of encouraging and facilitating efforts by the voluntary sector? Further, should government make use of its moral and legal authority to encourage the sort of institutions that tend to reduce the need for larger interventions by the state, such as marriage and the rearing of children within intact, two parent households? It happens to be the case that this was the direction our public policy was heading prior to September 11, 2001, when the war on terror became (justifiably) our national preoccupation. One of the great social liabilities of that event was the loss of momentum for a thoroughly edifying attempt at reducing the government's direct role in the inequality business and increasing its indirect role.

If we could return to that kind of public policy, we would not be giving up hope for a better way of life for all citizens. Rather we would be working to develop a low coercion model of the type suggested so far to bring about the good life for citizens.

The Government/Society Distinction

If we keep our idea of government's role in justice centered on the coercion of wrongdoers, punishment of wrong, and freedom for those who govern themselves, it will lead us back to a simple and valuable distinction set forth by Thomas Paine in *Common Sense*. In *Common Sense*, Paine distinguished between society and government.[19]

Society is the voluntary association of human beings. We rationally recognize that something such as building a house would take a very long time for a man working alone or might even be beyond his ability. But if he chooses to work with others, he may be able to have a habitable dwelling much faster. He can compensate the

---

19. Paine's widely read American Revolution–era tract is available in the public domain. One reliable place to find it is at http://www.constitution.org/tp/comsense.htm.

others with valuable goods he may possess or by giving his labor or knowledge to help with projects they may be interested in pursuing. Because of the much greater ability to live a good life by cooperating with other human beings, we choose to live in society. Society is a positive and voluntary enterprise that results in great blessings for those who participate in it.

Government, on the other hand, is different. Our vices create the need for government. While it is necessary, we must also fear that it will become a means of suffering.

The key to Paine's model is recognizing that society is the platform upon which we build our positive visions. It is voluntary with participants choosing to join and giving back in a reciprocal way so that they may continue to enjoy the benefits of society with others. Government is merely the remedy for bad behavior in society. It should be a corrector and a marker of boundaries rather than the engine of progress that drives civilization forward through constant application of force or the threat thereof. It is not well-suited to serve as the driver of advance because of the constant temptation to gain success by passing laws or gaining government favor rather than through real achievement. The ability to put together a block of votes is far from synonymous with competence in other critically important areas of social, commercial, and cultural improvement.

Thus, if we want to have a great society, then the way to achieve it is not to enact a program such as The Great Society, which was set forth by President Lyndon B. Johnson as a series of massive welfare programs in the form of payment to poor, single mothers of children, food stamps, and medical insurance for the poor and elderly. While the intent of the program is admirable, the overall merits have been debatable at best. Less charitably, we might note that the outcome was a vast increase in the size and powers of the government and substantial damage to the voluntary sector of society. If we keep Paine's distinction between society and government in mind, the program would better have been called The Great Government.

Society, by any measure, has taken quite a hit since the enactment of Johnson's programs in the 1960s. Far fewer children are born to a married mother and father today than was the norm at that time. The divorce rate is much higher. Many more women become pregnant without getting married. There are large segments of the populace in the lower socioeconomic registers in which married fatherhood has nearly disappeared as has the experience of the child seeing a father get up every day and go to work. Government assistance has become a much more important source of revenue for charitable social service providers and nonprofit entities such as colleges, hospitals, orphanages, rehabilitation programs, and a variety of others. It is also much less common to see multiple generations living in the same home. This, to some degree, is due to the expectation that seniors can make it on their own with social security and other government assistance. The federal government has gone from being primarily a defender of the nation (50 percent of revenues went to defense in 1960!) to being a provider of social services and entitlements (which are now by far the largest category of expenses in the budget). Critics of The Great Society are able to make a compelling case that it diminished cultural and social capital among the poor, established enduring cycles of poverty, and subsidized ways of life inimical to upward social mobility.

Through the growth of government, we have taken responsibility from the society sector and have transferred it to a giant, collective authority (a more friendly Leviathan). Though the goal is unquestionably benign, the outcome may not be.

Perhaps the best way to explain the problem is to highlight one of Aristotle's responses to his teacher, Plato. In *The Republic*, Plato hoped to illustrate the true nature of justice by enlarging the proper relationship of the reason, the will, and the appetite into a model of a whole community. In the community model, there is a class of guardians who are intended to care only for the city rather than for themselves and their particular interests. In order to facilitate that effort, the guardians are to be denied private property. Additionally, they will have no wives and children of their own. All property will be held in common, as will wives and children. The idea is that their only interest will be the general interest. They will care for everyone rather than for their own wives or their own children. On this plan, children might be said to be better off because instead of one set of parents, they will have thousands of attentive adults, all invested in their well-being.[20]

---

20. Plato outlines his ideas on this front in *The Republic*, sections 416d,e and 457d.

Whether the presentation of the guardian class was intended to be metaphorical or not, Aristotle chose to respond to Plato as though his proposal were a serious one. In his *Politics*, he wrote:

> What is common to the greatest number gets the least amount of care. People pay most attention to what is their own: they care less for what is common; or, at any rate, they care for it only to the extent to which each is individually concerned. Even when there is no other cause for inattention, people are more prone to neglect their duty when they think that another is attending to it.

Speaking specifically to the question of the family, he noted:

> [Under the plan of *The Republic*] each citizen will have a thousand sons; they will not be the sons of each citizen individually; any son whatever will be equally the son of any father whatever. The result will be that all will neglect all.[21]

In other words, the word *son* loses its meaning when abused in this fashion. The same is true of the concept of property. Utopian (or maybe dystopian) schemes that have attempted to displace traditional notions of family and property have failed even when backed by the full power of a totalitarian state.

The critical insight here is that human beings love the particular rather than the general. When we expand government and attempt to accomplish an ever-greater proportion of our social goals through its power, we go against the grain of human nature. In other words, we generalize. Family relationships, churches, local charities, and local connections all take on less importance as a purportedly omnicompetent state lays claim to collect and distribute a large (and getting larger) portion of resources. Individuals and local communities lose the joy, blessing, and accountability of right giving and helping as individual virtue generalizes into state provision. Recipients no longer have a tie with the giver, nor do they feel a strong need to respond properly to gifts and help by demonstrating that the aid has had an effect. Proper charity and assistance is degraded into the logic of entitlement. Being entitled is a much more comfortable place

---

21. Aristotle, *The Politics*, 1261b.

to be. It leads to poor stewardship of life and property and creates the conditions for the establishment of enduring cycles of poverty.

If government stays focused on its most critical functions relative to justice and order, then society must act to help bring those who need help along. In doing so, communities will discover that what John Stuart Mill said about localizing government as much as possible applies also to social responsibility for community improvement: to think and act is the equivalent of exercising muscles and helping them grow. Personal and social responsibility, located as near to the source as possible, develops the strength of citizens and of their communities. Moving that responsibility out into some distant Leviathan government results in the atrophy of virtue both among givers and recipients and to social atomization.

Conclusion

The Great Government does not produce a great society. A great society has the potential to develop in a political regime that focuses on the basic tasks of government while the voluntary sector flourishes. What is required is that we respect the idea of justice as coercion and restraint for those who do wrong and freedom for those who do no evil, while still remaining committed to making a better life for the people around us.

The first moves are the most immediate. If you are a child, be a respectful child who wants to learn and grow. If you are an adult, take care of your parents as they age. If you are a husband or wife, stay committed to your spouse. Work on sustaining a stable and peaceful household in which all the members feel heard, cared for, and respected. If you are a parent, focus on loving your child's other parent, providing financially and emotionally for the child, and encouraging the child in learning. If you are a grandparent, help young parents adjust to the newness of their role and encourage them in the hard work of taking care of children. If you live in a neighborhood, work on getting to know your neighbors and doing favors for each other. If you are a member of a church, focus less on what the church is doing to entertain you and spend time finding out how you can help others both in their quest to know God and by meeting needs in their daily lives. When you engage in business whether as a producer or customer, honor your contracts, pay your bills, and do not take advantage of others. God gives us many offices to occupy in this life. Were we to take all of them seriously, the need (and appetite) for government to fill voids might be far less great.

If we will take care of the many particulars of living together in society, the larger goods will follow in their wake. The church should be the alternate *civitas* leading the way as a kingdom of voluntary love and commitment.

One of the great questions of political philosophy has been whether government should concern itself primarily with small government in the form of something such as a mutual defense alliance, or whether it should instead be far more ambitious about achieving some great dream for all people. The question, it turns out, is a false one. Government is armed with the powers of coercion and force because it must be in order to do the job that God has given it, which is to frustrate the designs of those who would do evil. The broader society does not necessarily require those same weapons in order to achieve its goals. Nor is the use of those weapons well justified in many instances. We should be far keener to work in the voluntary sector than in the coercive one.

Two

BIG IMPLICATIONS FOR PUBLIC POLICY FROM SMALL-TOWN EXPERIENCE

S peaker of the House Thomas "Tip" O'Neill once memorably proclaimed that "all politics is local." He meant that successful politicians are the ones who never lose touch with local people and local concerns. In the two parts of this chapter, I look to the local to illuminate public policy at the national level. Specifically, I consider, first, the experience my maternal grandfather (a fellow I called "Pop") had working for the Postal Service as a mail carrier and, second, my own time working for a man who owned a small business in the same town. The setting is Decatur, Alabama, which is a blue-collar, industrial town on the banks of the Tennessee River, but the policy implications are national. The bottom line? Culture and character matter a great deal. Government efforts do not amount to much unless you have a good stock of social capital.

What It Takes to Make a Government-Jobs Strategy Pay Off

Daniel Patrick Moynihan (the longtime Democratic senator from New York) once suggested instituting twice-daily mail service as a way of providing good government jobs for African American males. Moynihan's notion demonstrates that modern liberals do not always build up the number of government jobs because more employees are needed to accomplish some mission, but because they are trying to provide a quality lifestyle for large numbers of people. In other words, the job itself (the entry on the payroll) is the mission.

In his response to President Obama's 2012 State of the Union address, Indiana governor Mitch Daniels commented that the president appears to sincerely believe that a middle class can be created with government jobs paid for by government dollars. Perhaps the president's position would not seem so fantastic if there were a different spiritual core at the heart of the liberalism of the modern Left.

Today, it appears that the US Postal Service (USPS) is unnecessary. It loses large amounts of money, partly because e-mail and digital imaging have made some of its former functions obsolete and partly because it has good competitors in the form of UPS and FedEx. The old argument that the USPS must exist to serve rural areas has lost force because the nation is more thickly populated now. Besides, the government could simply subsidize private carriers to serve outlying areas at a much cheaper cost than that of sustaining current USPS operations.

It is unlikely that the federal government will dissolve the USPS as a former necessity that has been bypassed by technology. The reason is that liberals are trying to accomplish something other than the delivery of the mail with the USPS. They are trying to create good livelihoods with solid salaries and benefits for a sizeable number of people. Such jobs, in theory, must be protected from the creative destruction and dislocations of capitalism.

The question is whether the modern liberal approach to improving the quality of citizens' lives by sustaining mass numbers of government jobs is workable. The answer is that it can be done (though at the cost of significant economic efficiency), but not with the mix of values currently accepted by modern liberals.

The Benefits of a Government Job

I have some personal history and inside knowledge to bring to bear on the problem. My maternal grandfather grew up in Cullman,

Alabama. His family was not well off, and he did not have much in the way of business assets or educational attainments to help him along. He married at a young age, found work in various factories, and began having children in Decatur, Alabama. The young family lived in a small home that he and his brothers built on a nice plot of land, right on the border of an industrial area and close to the Tennessee River.

Getting a job with the post office at about the age of thirty was a boon to him. Delivering the mail was a much cleaner, safer, and more comfortable job than working in factories, where he had once witnessed a tragic workplace accident resulting in the death of several men. It was the kind of accident that everyone present had realized was coming, and my grandmother recalled that he had nightmares about it for a long time after the event. He was more than ready to leave the industrial environment.

I can still remember seeing him in his postal uniform, making his rounds about town. He left early in the morning and got home in the afternoon. He was happy in that job. It provided for his family and gave him enough leisure time to begin an extensive avocation in horticulture.

One of the nice things about my childhood was the way he named various plants and flowers after family members. I very much enjoyed wandering around the greenhouses and nursery buildings he constructed on his property. My grandmother and my sister joined me for games of hide-and-seek. Any place was fair game as long as we did not disturb the flowers. There were lemons as large as grapefruit in his yard, and bees that sometimes loomed as fat as golf balls.

He became a fixture in our community as a longtime mailman and revered gardener. Each Christmas he received a hail of gifts and money from the people on his route. The walls of his home displayed a number of pictures and awards detailing his achievements at national flower shows, where he eventually became a respected judge.

Thanks to a government pension and benefits, he retired at about age sixty-two and spent the next quarter of a century pretty much doing what he wanted. He tended his flowers and spent time with his family. He kept working in the greenhouses and tending his plants until he was too weak to keep it up, as the consequences of a lifetime of smoking beset him. Moving to a more manageable home in the suburbs made him unhappy, but his loved ones had arranged it out of love and compassion for him and my grandmother.

We may not find a movie script in this story, but there is little doubt that his government job provided the income and working conditions for a pretty satisfying life. And here is the thing: He fulfilled his end of the bargain. What does that mean? I will explain.

Benefits with a Return

When, back in the 1960s, Moynihan first proposed expanding the number of Postal Service jobs, it is doubtful that he was merely hoping for a lot of people to be employed. He was too visionary for that. He was often considered a neoconservative, though he never voted like one. As the author of a much-cited study on the crisis of the black family, Moynihan knew of the importance of families for children. He likely hoped that all those new postal employees would do just what my grandfather did—that is, that they would live in such a way as to leverage the gift of a steady government job into something better for the next generation.

My grandfather—who had the very un-Waspy surname of Boike—was a Roman Catholic. He and my grandmother had five children in stair-step fashion. The seven-member family lived in a small house with three small bedrooms and one bathroom. The single lavatory had a bath with no shower. My grandmother was unable to drive due to a childhood eye injury, so the children had to walk to the Catholic school and any other activities they wanted to do. Trips to the grocery store had to wait until my grandfather could get home to take his wife out to get what she needed. She prepared virtually all of the meals for the family of seven.

He had three daughters and two sons. The first daughter married a young man who went on to work for NASA and IBM. The second child, a son, spent decades working for AT&T. He started as a line-man and worked his way up into the professional technology ranks. The second daughter, my mother, married a man who would work for thirty years at the Monsanto Corporation as a chemical engineer and who continues to do technical work at age seventy. The second son worked as a manager in retail throughout his career. And the third daughter, his fifth child, married a fellow who became an information technology executive.

The family grew up in the Catholic Church. Somehow they managed to afford private grade school for all five children. They were involved in their parish and were regular attendees at Mass.

There are a couple of things worth observing in the history of my family with my grandfather, the postman, at its head. First, notice the number of children he and his wife had: five. From their marriage came five households that jumped from blue-collar work to white-collar careers and families. Certainly, he received a government pension and benefits, which he used for a quarter century, but he had enough children growing up to take their places as taxpayers to support his retirement.

Second, consider the types of families the second-generation households became. There were no divorces, no out-of-wedlock births, no failures to finish school, no incarcerations, and steady records of employment. My grandfather's government job and the living it provided to his family acted like a lever that significantly improved the prospects of his children. But the job alone did not do that work; the other major factors were the Christian faith and the expectations he and his wife passed on to their children. Their stable, one-paycheck household led to the formation of several other stable, employed households that have paid a tremendous amount in taxes through the years.

Necessary Conditions

The kind of government policy that sets out to create lots of good government jobs (sometimes jobs that could be done by the private sector) that pay workers a nice wage and that provide them with a lengthy retirement with pension and benefits is only sustainable under certain conditions.

First, and most obviously, there must be a sizeable base of taxpayers *not* dependent on the government. Redistribution through government jobs relies upon a thriving private sector generating substantial profits and growing in size in order to fund the practice. If this dynamic does not hold, it is simply true that the redistributor will eventually, as Margaret Thatcher has pointed out, run out of other people's money.

Second, and equally as clear, if we set up a system in which large numbers of people will be receiving government pensions and benefits during long retirements, then we must have a *much larger* number of people in the generations succeeding them who are able to pay taxes to support the retired class during their economically nonproductive years.

Third, if we wish to prevent the formation of a standing class of government employees who agitate endlessly for their own betterment through the contributions of the taxpayers, then we need government jobs to function as a platform for greater opportunities for the government employees and their children.

My grandfather paid back his government job and benefits by doing the work well, having lots of children, providing for them, ensuring a quality education for them, establishing a strong moral foundation through parenting and church attendance, and then seeing the kids off into successful marriages. I suspect that what he did is exactly the kind of generational arc the late senator Moynihan had in mind.

Commitments at Odds with Good Results

On the other hand, however, if we establish these jobs, and those who obtain them do *not* get married, do *not* form stable families, and do *not* successfully raise children to complete their educations, launch into careers, and have families of their own, then we will not have succeeded. Government work will simply be another way for the political class to redistribute funds and to form coalitions at a cost to everyone not savvy or connected enough to find a way to get a piece of the pie.

The Boike family was a Democratic family. It is primarily a Republican one now. But the old saw about the Democrats being different back then is absolutely true. Government jobs were intended to do what they did in the life of my grandfather and his family. It was a strategy of the populist Democrats that was successful, I would argue, as were many of the big infrastructure investments such as the Tennessee Valley Authority and NASA. These were government expenditures that added to the national balance sheet by making bigger things possible in the private sector.

Today's Left would like to see government jobs have a positive effect, too, but their modern commitments are at odds with those good things happening. Marriage? The modern Left denies the need for natural marriage as a foundation for the most stable and successful families. Remember the rage Dan Quayle inspired when he suggested that a popular fictional character on TV set a bad example by choosing single motherhood? And what about the wrath George W. Bush incurred when he dedicated tiny amounts of money in the budget to encouraging marriage among the poor?

How about the idea of having enough children to grow the economy and sustain taxpayer-funded retirements? The modern Left is committed to encouraging people to have fewer children rather than more. Environmentalism has trumped the old commitment to growth and development. Few remember that the old Left and union leaders consistently argued for increased production and industrial activity rather than less. The environmentalist Left has trumped the old labor Left. And the labor movement has transitioned from the private sector to the public one, with the result that its agitation merely siphons off more money from the private sector with fewer beneficial results.

More Social Capital Needed

The modern Left's commitments result in the diminution of social capital. We wonder why inner-city schools struggle while suburban ones do better. Though most people blame the lack of money, the truth is that many urban schools are well funded, such as the ones in Washington, D.C. It is simply easier to preside over a school full of children with married parents who model work, commitment, delayed gratification in pursuit of goals, and other positive behaviors. Culturally, if we run out of that kind of social capital, then we are trapped in a cycle of decline.

If we want a society that provides opportunities for social and economic improvement through government jobs, and that takes care of the elderly through pensions (i.e., social security), then we must opt for the kind of family ethics and dynamics (with regard to marriage, procreation, and child rearing) that will reward the investment rather than simply creating an entitled class. Government jobs can function well for America if they are used as a lever, but they will merely increase our indebtedness if the primary use of a government salary is to enable a person to consume.

President Obama and Bob Brunton, Local Pharmacist

My grandfather's government job and the subsequent effect of that job when combined with significant cultural capital is the first part of my Decatur story. The second has to do with my experience in the same city years later working for a small-business owner named Bob Brunton. The months I spent with Mr. Brunton taught me to appreciate the individuals who create and sustain small businesses as well as the virtues of relational, obligation-based charity.

In an attempt to cut down on the expense of college, I navigated the curriculum efficiently and managed to graduate in three and a half years. As a result, over two decades ago I went home to live with my parents for nine months before starting a graduate program in public administration. Starting over with a new program meant that I needed to save up some money for an apartment deposit and other expenses. For reasons I cannot recall, I visited a neighborhood drug store called the Brunton Drug Company. The proprietor, Bob Brunton, hired me to make deliveries and work the cash register as needed. In fact, Bob Brunton knew my grandfather, the mailman. That is probably why he hired me.

I almost quit the job before it began. Bob showed me the truck I would use to make deliveries. It was a Mitsubishi Mighty Max with a stick shift. I did not know how to drive a stick shift. I went home, downcast, planning to find a non-humiliating time to leave a note under the door explaining why I could not start the job. Instead, I talked with my dad. He and I went out to a big parking lot at Point Mallard and worked on my technique. I reported for work the next day. It is a good thing Bob did not ride along to see me driving his truck. It was not pretty. I also did not know my way around neighborhoods other than my own. Since this was before GPS and smartphones, I had to keep a map on the passenger seat next to me. Being a stick shift novice and needing to keep a map in view was not easy, but I learned and eventually became proficient at getting the job done.

My job with the Brunton Drug Company lasted several months. I worked right up until it was time to go to the University of Georgia. It was a great experience. I have always liked to ask questions of people with whom I work so that I can learn. Bob was willing to teach me a lot about his operation.

When I heard President Obama's comments about people who start businesses, how they did not do it by themselves, how they are not smarter, and how they do not work harder, I first recalled a piece Senator George McGovern wrote late in life about the challenges he encountered in running a small inn. The onetime standard-bearer of the modern Left was mystified with what he saw as an excess of regulation. Then, I thought about Bob Brunton. When he started his drug store, Bob had to take all the financial risk of failure. He had to stay open long hours each day, and worked weekends too, for years until he had a solid client base and could afford to work fewer hours. But even when I was there, Bob was putting in a lot of time. He did not take off for lunch. He just heated a little container in the microwave and kept going.

Over time, he extended his business to include a local branch of the Roche medical labs. Bob managed his drugstore and the medical lab at the same time. Each day, some of the medical lab work would come over to the pharmacy and we would stop and pitch in on labeling containers and sorting. He was very shrewd that way. He knew the big drug stores would continue to cut into his business and took steps to protect himself.

Bob Brunton worked hard. Bob Brunton took financial risks. And Bob Brunton was smart about the way he conducted his business. I am sorry to say that Bob did not live all that long after he retired. He had given a lot of himself to his work.

The president talked about how we cannot take credit because somebody helped us along the way. He was thinking mostly about the credit due to the state when he made that remark. I can tell you that Bob Brunton helped me. He made a big impression both in his work ethic and in how he treated me. On my final day, it was time to close the store. Bob and I were the only people still on the premises. He gave me my final paycheck. Then, he pulled out a second check. Before he gave it to me, he said, "This is not a gift. This is not a loan. This is an obligation. When you are successful someday and you can help a young person, I expect you to do it." He handed me a check for an additional $500. At that time, my pay for the part-time job was $120 a week.

Some might argue that this paean to Bob Brunton attributes too much credit to him as an individual. Is it not true that Mr. Brunton's intelligence was a gift from God? Is it not also true that Brunton, like other small-business owners, benefitted from the vast infrastructure that exists in our country?

I do not dispute that Bob Brunton received native gifts from God, but neither would I be quick to dismiss any credit he deserved for having developed as a spiritual and moral person during his lifetime. In the course of succeeding as a small-business owner, Bob Brunton demonstrated virtues of hard work, perseverance, and generosity in addition to the intelligence he possessed. But whether his success was a result of a gift from God or not, I would be very hesitant to follow where such reasoning could lead, which is to a conclusion that God-given gifts belong to the state in some way for it to direct or tax as its leaders see fit.

With regard to the question of success springing from infrastructure, it is certainly true that even a neighborhood store such as Mr. Brunton's benefitted from modern transportation that made it possible for products to be efficiently shipped to his establishment. But I wonder whether infrastructure and small business have something like a chicken-and-egg relationship. Going further, maybe it is actually somewhat obvious that small business is prior to infrastructure. The United States did not build its great system of roads and bridges and then say, "Come one and all business persons, we are open for business!" Rather, the government responded to real commercial demands made obvious by the growth of industry within its borders. Activities of risk taking and hard work generated the need for the infrastructure. One might well argue that the government would never have come to command such great resources had not business succeeded first.

As a man of the Left, the president justifiably prefers to emphasize the role of government. I concede that the role of government is important. But he really should not downplay the contribution of the small-business owners who do so much to make our country great. But if that is the case the president wants to make, he has a long way to go to convince me because I worked for Bob Brunton of Decatur, Alabama, who ran a drug store.

These two Decatur stories help to illustrate the value of a good society in which the role of intermediary institutions such as family and small enterprise is significant. My grandfather's life-changing job as a postal worker would not have had nearly the impact it ultimately had if he had not possessed the habits and virtues necessary to build a life out of the modest security and leisure it afforded him. His commitment to family meant that the job lifted generations rather than simply keeping him going as another *homo economicus*. In like manner, Bob Brunton's role as a small-business owner was magnified by the virtues he embodied and taught by example. Rather than looking to the state to provide for a young man with financial needs, he provided legitimate work, paid a suitable wage, and then went beyond the economic transaction to invest in his young worker and to insist that I accept the obligation to do likewise for another young person when the opportunity arose. There is a vast territory between man and the state. It matters greatly what fills that space.

Three

THE SOUL OF LIBERTY

Y ou can find a lot of interesting things on Twitter packaged
in pithy statements of no more than 140 characters. Some of
you may recall that in the aftermath of the 2009 election in Iran,
a number of protesters claimed the government tampered with the
results in order to stay in power. Twitter was a key channel that the
protesters used both to express their outrage and to receive support
from sympathetic westerners, many of whom shaded their profile
pictures green as a sign of solidarity. I happened upon a number of
short statements from students in Iran who asked for "FREEDOM ...
DEMOCRACY ... AND ... SECULARISM!"

Having studied the history of the West and having paid particular
attention to the question of religion and politics, this combination of
concepts struck me as an odd one. But it obviously resonates with
some of the Iranian students who repeatedly use the Internet to
call for this combination of political ideals. I find it again and again.
They seem to believe it is the formula for liberty. But do these ideals
belong together?

What the students in Iran are looking for is a new revolution. They
do not like the results of the earlier revolution in the 1970s. That

revolution produced the current theocratic regime by overthrowing a secular nationalist dictator, the Shah of Iran, and replacing his rule with that of the Muslim clerics.

Of course, the Shah, though a "secular" ruler, did not have a great appreciation for democracy and freedom. This fact alone should give the students pause in their automatic association of secularism with freedom and democracy. There really is nothing inherent in the nature of secularism that would correspond to freedom or democracy. Secularism simply means that religious values and ideas are considered extraneous to public life. It might produce freedom from religion, but not necessarily political freedom.

The clerics did not like the secular Shah because he diminished their influence and presided over a more culturally relaxed moral climate. He was primarily interested in governing in such a way that reinforced his own power rather than protecting any notion of rights and freedoms of the people. He was also basically friendly to the West. He governed based on his interest, which is a worldly thing to do. *Worldly*, by the way, is not a bad synonym for *secular*.

The theocratic regime, despite the early hopes of western liberals in the 1970s, is not better than the Shah's. Neither government has been good for the nation's people or for their rights. The current regime is irrationally bent on the destruction of Israel, has pushed hard to develop offensive nuclear capabilities, and is, in many ways, oppressive. Perhaps a new revolution, another try, might produce a happier result.

The question is, what kind of a revolution? What sort of models should we consider, particularly if we are thinking in terms of freedom, democracy, and secularism? If I had the opportunity to speak with these Iranian students who are yearning for a better government, I would urge them to consider the two most consequential revolutions of the last three hundred years as a way of testing the soundness of their assumption. Those would be the American and French revolutions, which both happened in the closing decades of the eighteenth century.

Except for an epochal event such as the birth of Christ, it would be difficult to find historic occurrences that continue to shape the world in which we live more than these two events have. The Chinese premier Zhou Enlai was supposedly once asked for his opinion of the

French Revolution. According to the story, he thought for a moment and said, "Too soon to tell." If the story is true, the assessment was correct. The French Revolution continues to have an effect on our history. What was started then impacts us in our own time. The French revolutionaries, in their hubris, set out to remake the world with a brand new calendar that would replace the old Christian division of history. Their calendar would begin with Year One, thus signifying the importance they attached to their own acts and ideas. Not so long ago, another group of revolutionaries in Cambodia, under the dictator Pol Pot, declared Year Zero, thinking their own efforts to be worthy of a new beginning of human history. Both of those revolutions, the French one and the Cambodian one, proved exceptionally bloody. Political execution, in both cases, was the primary method of achieving fundamental agreement.

The French crisis began when Louis XVI called in the Estates General representing the nobility, the clergy, and the people to help resolve a financial shortfall. Any voting was done by estates rather than by heads. Thus, the first and second estates (nobility and clergy) could stand together and impose their will (and the king's) on the third estate (the people). There were those who noticed the fixed nature of the game. The nobility was tied to the king. Many of the clergy were nobility themselves holding offices such as bishop because they were revenue-generating posts. Those two orders stood together. The vote of the third estate, the people, was irrelevant because it was one vote against the other two. A powerful pamphlet of the time stirred the people by exclaiming,

> What Is The Third Estate? Everything.
>
> What Has It Been Until Now In The Political Order? Nothing.
>
> What Does It Want To Be? Something.[1]

These democratic sentiments drove the beginning of the French Revolution. What was supposed to be a simple exercise in collecting greater revenue to support the king's activities blossomed into extreme political unrest and then full-on revolution.

---

1. Emmanuel Sieyès, *What Is the Third Estate?* (1789). This famous pamphlet has been frequently anthologized.

The common people (which included merchants and artisans, and not just peasants) were tired of bearing heavy financial burdens, doing most of the productive work in the society, and having no real say in the government of the French state. Top Catholic clergy lived lives of privilege and did not seem overly concerned with the well-being of the people. It was said of those members of the clergy that they administered more provinces than sacraments. The people saw a clerical elite that was more interested in preserving its own power and prerogatives and supporting the status quo than it was in either calling the state to righteousness or engaging in serious ministry.

France had an intellectual elite with a clear anti-Christian agenda. The famed Voltaire loved to provoke with his criticisms and mockery of the Christian view of God. Not quite as famously, he made sure to close the doors when he discussed these matters with his upper-class friends for fear that his servants, upon hearing his criticisms, would no longer feel bound by religious morality and would steal his silver. He and Rousseau, another proclaimer of the pernicious influence of Christianity, both died in the period shortly before the revolution occurred. Rousseau felt that the Christian church introduced a second master that would confuse the loyalties of citizens. Instead, he believed their hearts and minds would better be aligned directly with the general will of the people in the form of the state. The Frenchman Denis Diderot, mastermind of an encyclopedia designed to help liberate the minds of men, is said to have proclaimed his desire to see the last king strangled with the guts of the last priest.

And so, this was a revolution designed not merely to overturn the throne, but also to break the power of the altar. In relatively short order, the leaders of the revolution embarked upon a campaign of explicit dechristianization. Though they had begun working at first to gain control of the Catholic clergy in their nation, they moved more boldly to create an entirely new culture. The Cathedral of Notre Dame in Paris became the Temple of Reason. Over fourteen hundred streets were renamed to remove not only the names of monarchs, but also of saints and other reminders of the faith. Going further, the new republic established a civil cult around the worship of the Supreme Being. This fit well with Rousseau's concept of the general will. The new state called upon artists and writers to come up with new ways to celebrate special occasions in line with the new cult. In essence, the nation would be worshipping its collective self and its own values in true Durkheimian fashion.

In the beginning, there were great hopes for the revolution. But in the heady rush of making the world new with the power of unfettered human reason, something went terribly wrong. Mark Noll captured it well when he wrote, "Escape from deference, traditions, and the rule of hereditary elites led to new sources of oppression rather than a flowering of liberty. Indiscriminate violence orchestrated by new rulers mocked visions of equality."[2] The leaders first executed hundreds and then many thousands. Their actions foreshadowed the new totalitarian states of the twentieth century, which liquidated millions for failure to unquestioningly follow grand visions with new ideas about human life and the destiny of states.

At this point, it is well to recall the late Richard John Neuhaus' observation that those who believe that the record of the secular Enlightenment is spotless compared to that of the church are essentially in denial. "Those who tell the story this way overlook the fact that in three hundred years the Inquisition had fewer victims than were killed any given afternoon during the years of Stalin's purges and Hitler's concentration camps."[3] He could easily have added Mao's violent Cultural Revolution that empowered crazed teenagers to beat senior citizens with belt buckles if they showed signs of lacking sufficient zeal. The story of the French Revolution was much the same. The loss of life, not in any war, but in furtherance of the domestic, ideological ambitions of a state, far outstripped any deaths caused by the Inquisition.

The rulers of the new France were men like Robespierre and the ironically named Committee of Public Safety. It was they who preceded the Nazis of the twentieth century in justifying their actions out of "love for the fatherland." The revolution met the end that radical, utopian efforts often do. Robespierre died when the guillotine separated his head from his body. France fell into crisis and disorder that had to be resolved. As so often happens, a strong man stepped

---

2. Mark Noll, *Turning Points: Decisive Moments in the History of Christianity* (Grand Rapids: Baker Books, 1997), 249.

3. Richard John Neuhaus, *The Naked Public Square: Religion and Democracy in America* (Grand Rapids: Eerdmans, 1984), 94.

in. Napoleon became the absolute ruler of France and proceeded to bring war and death like a plague to much of Europe. The ultimate fruit of the revolution was an unstable France that did not become a solid constitutional republic until years after the Second World War when General de Gaulle was able to name his conditions for taking power and forming a workable government.

We have briefly considered the French Revolution, a secularizing revolution, a revolution that sought to wipe out what had gone before and to remake the world in the name of human reason free from the chains of either monarchical command or religious enslavement. The result was similar to letting a twelve-year-old drive the car on a busy interstate after he has loudly criticized his parent for two hours: shaky, risky, and in this case, fatally dangerous. The once hopeful social movement ended in dictatorship. Based on the French Revolution and on revolutions that to some degree followed in its footsteps—the Russian Revolution, the Chinese Communist Revolution, and, yes, Pol Pot's revolution in Cambodia, all of which were fully secular—the case for naturally associating freedom, democracy, and secularism is not very good.

Can one make a case that freedom and democracy go with something other than secularism? Might one propose that Christianity bears some responsibility for fostering freedom and democracy in the world? For the answer, one must consider the American Revolution, which is different from its European counterpart in a number of ways. The differences are made more striking by the closeness in time of the two revolutions and by the alliance of the Americans with the French nation (then controlled by the crown) during the American Revolutionary War.

The American Revolution was different in part because the American church situation was so different from anything in Europe. In France, the Catholic Church had maintained power despite the Reformation because the Huguenot Henry of Navarre converted to Catholicism in order to take the throne, declaring, "Paris is worth a mass." But even in the European countries where the Reformation prevailed, the church tended to align itself with the monarchy if for no other reason than to protect itself from Rome, which was willing to fight for what it considered to be its rights.

Crowned heads often welcomed the Reformation. Their motives varied. Some favored the birth of Protestantism because of their own Christian piety. Others embraced it because the Reformation had the effect of reducing the power of the papacy and enhancing their own independence as rulers. (Unfortunately, that result of the Reformation was not a happy one as it led to the growth of absolutism in Europe as leaders were less often checked by the power of the church.) Ultimately, each nation in Europe chose a national church and established it legally, sometimes Catholic and sometimes Protestant.

The American situation did not fit the traditional European pattern of one nation, one people, and one church. It might be illustrative to tell a story from when I was a graduate student at the University of Georgia many years ago. One of my peers was a British punk rock sort of a fellow with an honest-to-goodness mohawk and a goatee. When he found out I was a Christian (probably by looking at some provocative T-shirt I was wearing), he explained to me that England is perfect and asked whether I wanted to know why. "England is perfect," he said smiling, "because we shipped all of our criminals out to Australia and our religious *fa-na-tics*"—that is how he pronounced it—"to America." We shared a good laugh because, like most things we find funny, there is some truth to it.

We all know the story of the religious dissenters (the Puritans) who came to the wild frontier in America to worship in their own way. We think of them as promoters of religious liberty. That is a misperception. They wanted to set up a church with the doctrines they believed were right and then to enforce adherence to those doctrines. Their church was intended for everyone in the community. Those who disagreed, such as, for example, Roger Williams, were forced out of the fellowship, both spiritually and politically. In early America, the original design was in favor of a legal relationship between the church and state. Religious freedom did not come to America because of the desire of Puritans to be free, nor did it come because intellectuals like Thomas Jefferson dreamed it up. It would be more accurate to say, as the great historians of American Christianity have noted, that conditions on the ground brought religious liberty, perhaps providentially.

The combination of the reality of frontier life, vast geographic spaces lightly populated, the remoteness of European religious sponsors and authorities, and the simple fact of religious pluralism led to religious liberty in America. Certainly, there were various church establishments, as with Congregationalists and Episcopalians, but they were less imposing than the original European arrangements and they coexisted with other colonies (and later states) that openly embraced religious toleration of a variety of confessions.

Some varieties of American Christians pushed for religious freedom as a matter of their understanding of the faith itself. They saw the state as a merely instrumental and temporal authority with no right to legal authority over religious observance. That right was God's alone. One of the greatest contributions of the Baptist faith, for instance, was its insistence that the regenerate church is better than the comprehensive church. In other words, the Baptists believed participation in the church should be voluntary and not some community mandated enterprise.

In addition to the unique landscape of American Christianity due to religious pluralism and increasing toleration, there was also the gigantic impact of the Great Awakening of the early eighteenth century. Pre–Revolutionary War America was post–Great Awakening America. This is one of the reasons it is strange to hear some writers claim that the America of the founding was largely irreligious. The Awakening, sparked by the sensation of the public preaching of George Whitefield, resulted in the largest community gatherings in colonial history.

One need not demonstrate immediate causation between the Awakening and the American Revolution in order to see that the Awakening helped change American Christianity. Instead of the old pattern of a highly educated clergy formalistically conveying the faith to a deferential flock, American religion began to be dominated by a new sense of direct experience between God and the individual believer. Foreshadowing the later massive success of Baptists and Methodists in the nineteenth century, earnest sincerity, enthusiasm, personal empowerment, and energetic commitment began to be the hallmarks of the faith in America. By the time of the American Revolution, the church had a degree of independence not seen on the

Continent across the ocean. The willingness of Americans to challenge ancient and foreign authority was as great as it had ever been.

When American colonists began to feel alarmed at English laws, which seemed to overreach into the affairs of people accustomed to governing themselves, and seemed to do so without offering them any representation in the process, the American church joined the popular protest movement. The New England clergy, if anything, may have been too enthusiastic about challenging the English. Unlike the French Catholic Church, the American church was a major force in the revolution rather than a target of it.

The American Revolution did not have the secularizing agenda of the French Revolution. Certainly, the two revolutions were similar in their distaste for monarchy and power exercised in an arbitrary fashion without regard for the natural rights of citizens. In almost all other respects, the two revolutions were worlds apart. They differed on the matter of secularization and had hugely different results. One revolution led to dictatorship. The other led to the expansion of freedom and democracy.

So far, I have sought to demonstrate how different the religious pluralism and voluntary Christianity of America was in comparison with the established church of France, which was intertwined with the throne to the point of being an object of the revolutionaries' scorn. While the French revolutionaries dechristianized their nation, the same idea considered in the context of American society during the same period would have been ridiculous. By and large, the American church was with the popular movement of the people. Yet, contrary to the assumption of the Iranian student that freedom, democracy, and secularism go together, it was the much more Christian American Revolution that led to the creation of the longest running and most stable constitutional republic of the last two millennia.

In examining the broader question of whether freedom, democracy, and secularism naturally go together, there is more to say than that the French Revolution was secularizing in intent, but *did not* result in freedom and democracy, and that the American Revolution was not secularizing and *did* result in the expansion of freedom and democracy. To say that much would be simply to observe covariation. In other words, I would be able to say that freedom, democracy, and

Christianity traveled together in the American Revolution while freedom, democracy, and secularism did not travel together in the French Revolution. So far, I have some evidence. The occurrence of two or three things together is a powerful testimony. For example, when lightning hits nearby, within a short time we hear the boom of thunder. We might begin to suppose that the strike of the lightning is the cause of the thunder. Therefore, in what follows, I will look in more detail at the relationship of Christianity to freedom and democracy.

The most basic question in politics has to do with power. In the ancient world—indeed, in the modern world—many political rulers exercised power as though they were given it *carte blanche* by a god or as though they themselves were invested with divine substance. That can be seen in the Roman emperors, who were worshipped as gods, and also in various Asian emperors of more recent vintage who were supposedly divine. These nations and peoples embraced their own Hobbesian Leviathans in exchange for peace and order. Such a rule was often achieved via conquest.

In the French Revolution, the battle was over who had the power. The revolutionaries forcibly took power from the king and the nobles and gave it, at least in name, to the people. In reality, the power was held by men like Robespierre and the Committee of Public Safety. Power held in the name of the people is often the most dangerous of all. The use of such power can often be a cynical and oppressive exercise benefitting from the illusion of moral authority—"We rule in the name of the people!" The dictator Castro, for example, has ruled in the name of the people. Little freedom and democracy have accompanied his secularism.

The French Revolution aimed to take the power away from an elite and give it to the people who would then all gladly bow to what Rousseau called the general will. Because the Christian church might clash with the general will and set up a conflict in the individual citizen's mind, the church would be better left out of the society. This is secularism at its core. Religious convictions interfere with the operation of a state empowered to enforce the general will. Too many fail to realize that religion can be a check on state power, one that is often freedom-enhancing, especially if that religion is Christianity.

The special genius of the American Revolution and of the American founding was to see that, while it was important to be right about the question of who wields power, another question is at least equally important. And that question is: *How much* power is available to the state? The American Revolution was a response to a perceived abuse of power and the American founding revolved around limiting power so that it would be more difficult to abuse. Why might they have been concerned with that?

Let us begin with a look at who the Puritans were. The Puritans were Calvinists and were certainly powerful shapers of the American mind. A story that is often missed when we think about early America is just how powerfully Calvinist it was in nature. One of the hallmarks of Calvinism is its emphasis on the fallen nature of human beings. This doctrine punctures personal pride and helps foster a tremendous suspicion of power in human hands. And rulers are no different than any other human beings. They are fallen. Original sin and human fallenness are doctrines that naturally underwrite the ideas of limited government and constitutionalism.

One might also think of the church father Augustine (often tied to Calvin to the point that some Calvinists have at times called themselves Augustinians) in this connection. Because he saw sinful pride as the source of men ruling over men, and because of his acute awareness of the self-serving nature of human beings, Augustine had a dark view of the state. Without Christ, it could not truly know justice. The state might be no better than the largest and most well-equipped band of robbers lining their own pockets with the fruit of oppression and tyranny.

The United States Constitution, more than any other, is an acknowledgment of the problem of original sin. Power is checked, limited, and balanced to the point that you could describe our government as an engine with sand in the gears. It purposely clashes and grinds. You can see that even when the president has an enormous advantage in the Congress, he has a hard time pushing his agenda through. That difficulty is part of the design. You can see the spirit of American Christianity in that design. You can see Calvinism in it. You can see the skepticism toward state power.

More generally, consider the Christian idea of humanity as created in the image of God. A person created in the image of God is a good prospect to be the holder of inalienable rights. Christian anthropology lends credence to a view of human beings as having a certain dignity not subject to the whim of governments. Neither kings nor a population wielding the general will should be capable of disturbing a person's essential rights and liberties. The notion of persons as bearers of the image of God also provides a basis for human equality. And equality supports democracy.

The Bible itself also played a role in fostering democracy in the West, and certainly in America. As I make that claim, I am aware that the text of the Bible deals primarily with monarchy. To support my contention that the Bible helped bring democracy to the world, I am thinking of a broader method than one that merely pulls out a biblical passage. Consider the Bible as a cultural force. Since the time of the Reformation, the biblical text has been widely available in the vernacular of civilized peoples. It has long been viewed by readers as a source of both the revelation of God's plan and general teaching on right and wrong. For political purposes, you could say that it offers the community equivalent of an objective standard of right and wrong. In the wake of the Bible's wide availability and the Reformers' drive for literacy among the people, it became popular to say that a ploughboy with the Scripture on his side could challenge a prelate. This, too, had a democratizing effect. Two people, be they ploughboy or prelate, stood equal before the word of God. Social or legal position could not decide a dispute where the Bible spoke clearly.

As we begin to put some of these ideas together, we have a pretty strong foundation (and, more important, a foundation widely accepted by the people) for freedom (the kind of freedom that arises from limited government, constitutionalism, and inherent rights and liberties) and democracy. Perhaps our Iranian students should consider whether they might find a more lasting solution to their troubles in freedom, democracy, and Christianity.

To be fair, I would be remiss if I left readers with the impression that the Christian faith is the sole source of some of these critical features of the American brand of democracy and ordered liberty. It is not. Another major inspiration for the American founding was the Roman Republic. There, too, one could find things like checks and balances, a degree of democracy, and the separation of powers. It is a fault of some scholars that they want to give all the credit to classical sources (referring to the Greco-Roman world) rather than Christian ones. I will not make the same mistake in reverse.

It would be better and more accurate to say that our enduring and successful constitutional republic was founded by Americans drawing from both sources (which is a point Michael Novak has made). One can effectively derive support for freedom and democracy from the Christian tradition without reference to the Greco-Roman precedents, but it would be wrong to suggest that our Constitution was inspired in that way. The American founding was a fusion of Christian and classical sources. Happily, the Christian influence successfully modifies some of the worst elements of the classical tradition, such as a deficit of virtues like humility, mercy, and compassion.

What I do think is incontestable is that the strong Christian influence came simply from citizens living in an American culture thoroughly permeated with the Bible and the church in various manifestations. At the popular level there was no contest: The Christian faith was the greater influence by far. The Bible was the one book everyone owned and most read.

The Christian view of humanity promotes these things that the Iranian student wants, while the Muslim view of humanity, with which the Iranian student is more familiar, does not. And I think *that* is why young Iranians are calling for secularism. It is not because there is any great evidence that secularism is productive of freedom and democracy. Instead, it is because the only way they can envision getting there is if they pretend their faith does not matter. That is what secularism encourages us to do.

My friend Louis Markos, who is a wonderful scholar of the humanities, read my earlier thoughts on this matter and summed things up in the following way. In the Muslim world, the church *is* the state. In the French Revolution, and in those other secular revolutions to which I referred, the state is the church. In other words, the state generates moral values on its own and then enforces them. In the early history of the American republic, the founders and the people managed to thread history's needle (providentially) and arrived at an almost ideal separation of church and state.

For this arrangement, I think a great deal of credit must go to Martin Luther and John Locke, who correctly understood that the church must not rule souls by steel, and to the Baptists, who insisted on voluntary participation in the church. But this separation would not mean that the church would withdraw from the life of the society. No. Instead, the church in America has been free and vital. The church is a huge influence on the values of the culture. The church works to help the state when it is right and calls the state to righteousness when it is wrong. *The church is the soul of the system.*

But still, the Iranian student and others are likely to say: Why not just leave out the church? Why not leave out that Christian particularity that you insist is so important to culture? Why can we not just have the freedom and democracy and ignore the rest? Fine, the faith may have helped us reach this point, but I do not know why we need it now. We have evolved socially and politically.

The simplest answer is to invoke Elton Trueblood's magnificent metaphor of the cut-flower civilization. A flower grows and becomes beautiful because it is rooted in the ground where it can access the things it needs to live, such as nutrition and water. The roots are life. If you cut the flower at its stem and put it in a vase, it will remain beautiful for a time, but it will die and decay. What was beautiful will be lost.

Our civilization is like the flower. The flower did not simply arrive fully formed and beautiful. It grew and developed over time in response to certain events (such as rain, sun, and wind) and in connection with a source, which was the fertile ground. The things that we value in our civilization also grew and developed in response to certain events and in connection with a source, which in the West has largely been the Bible. If we separate ourselves from that source and simply declare ourselves to be appreciators of things like freedom and democracy, a question arises: Why do we believe in those things and not in others? What were the reasons that we came to believe in those things in the first place? If we no longer believe those reasons to be valid, then are the concepts we embraced valid?

Civilization, particularly our kind of civilization, is far more vulnerable than we would like to believe, especially if we turn our backs on God—especially if we turn our backs on a God who intervened in history.

Four

TROUBLES WITH SECULARISM

It is probably true that historically the primary model for the interaction of religion and politics has been for the two forces to be unified: one ruler, one religion, and one people aligned with both. If we view secularism as the abandonment of that system, then secularism has become dominant in most places other than in Islamic theocracies such as Iran.

I do not think, however, that the abandonment of the system I have described can be attributed to the triumph of secularism, although that is a common narrative. I will try to map out the religio-political landscape in this chapter.

Secularism is the public philosophy that religion should be confined to its own sphere, which is to say that it should be a private matter for individuals and small subcommunities. For some, secularism is very desirable. They do not want to see public matters shaped by religious sensibilities. In other words, secularism is about more than the severing of church-state ties and the removal of religious symbols from public buildings and property. Secularism goes further in attempting to create an expectation that religious thought and belief should have no place in public discourse or in many other human activities such as science, business, law, or war.

Running parallel to secularism is the sociological theory of secularization, which holds that human beings are leaving religion behind as they gain knowledge about the world scientifically and culturally. On this view, human beings have used religion as an explanation for physical phenomena of the world they could not understand. As science provides its own explanations about how the natural world functions, religion inevitably retreats to ever-diminishing epistemological real estate. Another version of the same idea is that no one could use electricity and still believe in miracles. Science completely displaces the supernatural. (I confess that I have always found it difficult to understand the supposed power of this argument. The existence of electricity, for example, really tells me nothing about whether I have a soul or whether there is a God to whom I might relate.)

At the same time, thanks to telecommunications and the ease of international travel, modern humans have a far greater awareness of the diversity of religious belief around the world and thus must find themselves less certain of their spiritual convictions. Peter Berger helped describe this phenomenon with the phrases "structures of plausibility" and "the sacred canopy."[1] In a society with fewer foreign entrants and a stable culture not suffering challenges and incursions, it is easy to believe the cultural religious story. The structures of plausibility are firmly in place and undisturbed. The society dwells beneath a sacred canopy. Modernity, however, has been full of disruptions and challenges to the old structures. It is harder to maintain a religious belief with doubters all around than it is when one is surrounded by fellow believers. Observing the fundamental dynamic at work around 1970, Berger once told the *New York Times* that the year 2000 would find only tiny groups of believers huddled together against the onslaught of modernity. In defense of Professor Berger, I should note that he revised his views well before the turn of the millennium!

The reality is more complicated and interesting than a mere clash between secularism and religion. Religion is not alone in facing constant challenges because of the nature of the modern world. It is worldviews in general that are under siege. When we are surrounded

---

1. Peter Berger, *The Sacred Canopy: Elements of a Sociological Theory of Religion* (New York: Anchor Books; Doubleday, 1969).

by people with whom we agree, it is easier to maintain beliefs about the world and the values that are important. We are in the middle of a terrific contest of various orthodoxies, which are not merely religious. The primary arena is political because government is now so large and attempts to do so many things. This contest, however, has not destroyed political beliefs or other values simply by constantly challenging them. The same is true for religious thinking and devotion. They persist, and far more strongly than the secularization theorists thought they could.

For example, one may notice that it is easier for those of us who are conservatives to hold our political beliefs while gathered together at a place like Hillsdale College, but of course we do not simply jettison those beliefs when we find ourselves in different surroundings such as Washington, D.C., or the University of Wisconsin–Madison. Hillsdale-ian beliefs persist in the face of disagreement because those who embrace them have good reason to maintain their position. They still find those beliefs to be a superior account of political and cultural matters than the ones that confront them in more liberal climes. In the same way, religious belief will not be eliminated simply by the presence of alternative accounts of God's existence.

Sometimes political beliefs persist against all evidence! How many communists remain in the world? I suspect it is a reasonably large number. Indeed, there are some even in places like China and Russia who are sentimental about its reign, despite the failure of the project.

In his intellectual autobiography, Berger told an interesting and illustrative story. During the Cold War, he introduced a female friend supportive of the Soviet Union to a Latvian couple who told horror stories about what they had experienced at the hands of Communist enforcers. The young woman put her hands over her ears and said she did not want to hear any more. Afterward, she admitted she did not think they were lying but added that she felt there was probably some additional information that would change everything they said. She said she would check it out. Berger never saw her again.

I tell that story for a couple of reasons. First, it demonstrates that the difference between politics and religion is often not very large, despite how confidently some secularists claim to separate the two. Second, it shows that secularization theory may have limited its focus too much by isolating religion. One might have to broaden the picture to include the larger set of human beliefs, which are rationally underdetermined, in order to be more accurate.

Peter Berger and others have moved from a secularization paradigm to one based on pluralism. Modernity produces pluralism, but pluralism does not necessarily produce secularism. People are simply in a position today to choose their faith rather than taking it for granted. There is nothing about that situation that guarantees a secular future. Instead, we have a huge swath of social life that is rationally underdetermined and highly contested. There are many participants in the contest of worldviews. Some of them are religious. Others have a more secular orientation. And, of course, shades of religion or irreligion are far from being the only vectors involved. There are questions of freedom, solidarity, humanity's use of the natural world, relations between the sexes, and many other questions. We are slowly coming to realize that taking religion out of the equation does not eliminate the contest of worldviews. It merely provides an artificial leg up to some perspectives while penalizing or inhibiting others. This realization has contributed to the development of postmodernism. If secularism reflects disappointment with the social experience of public religion, postmodernism reflects disappointment with secularism, or perhaps a loss of confidence in its ability to provide the neutral ground of greater social enlightenment.

Here again, I think Berger is instructive. It is true that reality is, to some degree, socially constructed. But that does not mean there are no facts. There are empirical facts. There are social facts. They are open to interpretation, but not all interpretations are equal. If nothing exists but narratives, then we are like schizophrenics unable to distinguish between reality and fantasy. The answer is not to give up, but, as John Stuart Mill counseled, to allow the most free and fair debate possible in search of the truth. No other process contains as much promise.

To say that secularization is not inevitable is not to do away with the idea of secularism entirely. Secularization theorists attempted to offer a scientific prediction about the persistence of religion in society. But secularism is not so much about prediction as it is about a prescription for how human beings should live together.

It is important to draw a sharp line between the separation of church and state on the one hand and secularism on the other.

Secularists frequently present their view of politics and religion in terms of the separation of church and state. I believe that is a mistake on their part. The separation of church and state, in the classical sense, means that the state does not control the church, nor does the church control the state. They are financially independent of one another. Church ministers are not paid employees of the state. Neither does the state levy a tax for the support of the church. Members of the state are not automatically presumed to be members of the church. In a society where the separation of church and state exists, the church can be described as regenerate (or voluntary) rather than comprehensive, which was the old model.

The features I have listed so far are identical to what would exist in a secularist state, but with an important difference. The separation model implicitly concedes a special role for the church. The dividing line is as much intended to protect the church from political interference and corruption as it is to prevent religious imposition on citizens. It must be remembered that separation was driven as much by serious Christians as it was by figures, such as Thomas Jefferson, who were less concerned with spiritual devotion.

The other major difference between separation and secularism is that classical separation does not contemplate the privatization of religion and the removal of it from the public square. One of the great American thoughts has been that religion can edify and sustain democracy. As Philip Hamburger demonstrated in his book *Separation of Church and State*, the notion that faith would be isolated from the functioning of the republic was disturbing to many in the founding generation, just as it is to many Christians today.[2] This conference between faith and the proper functioning of the republic was evident in Washington's assertion in his Farewell Address that religion and morality are the "indispensable supports" of "political prosperity."

Under the separation model, the influence of religion is unofficial, but real. The church should be the church and the state should be the state, but the church's work is to call both citizens and the state to be righteous and to do justice. In other words, part of the church's task is to call the state to *be the state*, which God has ordained for

---

2. Philip Hamburger, *Separation of Church and State* (Cambridge, MA: Harvard University Press, 2002).

the good of men and women. Separation involves a much richer role for the church than mere secularism.

In the preceding chapter, I noted that young Iranians have recently called for freedom, democracy, and secularism. I think they actually mean that they would like to see something more like the separation of church and state. Of course, the great question is whether something like the separation of church and state is consistent with Islam. In the case of Christianity, separation is arguably part of the genetic code of the faith. That is, Christianity permits earthly kings to provide only earthly justice and order during the time before the return of Christ, who is the world's one true lord. Christ himself appeared to acknowledge a place for temporal kingdoms when he contemplated Caesar's image on a coin (Matt. 22:15–22).

So, what has secularism looked like in the modern world? The most aggressive type presented itself in the form of social leveling. It is a term that has previously been used in a mostly economic sense, but which I think had farther-reaching implications in the efforts of the totalitarian super-states of the twentieth century.

Social leveling is something that we typically associate with the destruction of material differences between human beings. It is the socialist dream of a classless society in which distinctions, usually the result of economic variation, are made irrelevant. The state, empowered by the political action of the masses (or at least a group claiming to speak for the masses), works to gain control of the wealth and property of a society and then to redistribute it in such a way as to make people equal. It should be obvious that this type of action vastly increases the power of the state because, as Milton Friedman has pointed out, the state that determines a person's economic destiny can easily dictate political opinions to that person.

The logic of social leveling applies to more than property. Indeed, socialism and a species of secularism can be closely related to one another. While socialism seeks to erase the economic distinctions between human beings by taking individual choices about property out of people's hands, secularism seeks to erase the religious differences between people by making religion irrelevant to the life of the community. This action of secularism, so similar to socialism, is why I refer to it as a type of social leveling.

Social leveling has a degree of appeal. Equality is a goal worth striving for. Considered conceptually, this can be a beautiful thing. In David Horowitz's book *Radical Son*, he wrote about growing up as the child of Communists and attending Camp Wo-Chi-Ca (Workers' Children's Camp) in the summers. In one of the book's more poignant moments he described how his father found apparent acceptance among fellow revolutionaries. Consider this excerpt from his father's journal: "Three Russians in the cabin. One small, second fat, third big and bony. All three smiling, friendly and talkative but not humble. Wishing to learn the Russian for 'I am,' I asked the small one how to say 'I am a Jew.' He said, 'No Jew, no Christian. After Communism, *all people*.'"[3]

The beauty of that moment depends greatly upon the person participating in it and the insistence with which he is told there will be "no Jew, no Christian," only "people." On the one hand, the statement could be a poetic paean to the brotherhood of man. On the other, it could be the declaration of a serious determination to wipe out religious differences by whatever means necessary. Regrettably, the latter turned out mostly to be the case. The most ambitious dreams of establishing human equality have tended to degenerate into terrors exercised toward freedom. The social levelers of aggressive secularism failed to adequately appreciate that a man or woman might want to be a Christian, for example, out of his or her desire to pursue the truth about God and the world. Revolutionaries too often simply assumed faith identities were like tribal tattoos that needed to be wiped out of existence, by force if necessary.

Ultimately, the great totalitarian experiments either failed, as in the case of the Soviet Union, or radically changed course, as in the case of the Chinese. We do not see aggressively secular superstates seriously attempting to dictate the complete package of faith (or non-faith) and worldview to their citizens as these nations once did. The most notorious example, North Korea, is a renegade state tenuously connected to the family of nations by its periodic threats and demands. At least in the West, the attempt to enforce religious uniformity, first by the religio-political establishments and then by

---

3. David Horowitz, *Radical Son: A Generational Odyssey* (New York: Touchstone, 1997), 19.

the totalitarian program of official atheism or cynical ownership of the church by the state, seems to have largely passed into history.

Totalitarian, aggressive secularism of the European and Asian type did not strike an equally powerful chord in the United States, even though it achieved substantial victories in Mexico just to the south. The key difference for America was the nature of its revolution. In the French Revolution, as we have seen, the struggle was against the combined unit of the throne and the altar. In America, largely because of the vast Atlantic Ocean separating churches from sponsors in Europe, and because of other conditions on the ground that contributed to Christian pluralism and religious toleration, the churches were not wedded to the crown. Some have argued that the ministers of New England were perhaps too enthusiastic about the idea of revolution! Americans threw off the yoke of European monarchy, but this rejection did not entail resentment against the church.

The difference became clear as the French Revolution developed a few years after its American predecessor. At first, Americans were somewhat inclined to cheer the French effort. But as they realized that the French Revolution was not merely anti-clerical or anti-Catholic, but also fundamentally anti-Christian, American support declined dramatically.

For most of the nineteenth century in America the connection between Christianity and the culture of the United States was powerfully reaffirmed. Edwin Gaustad has argued that the Bible maintained a position of central symbolic status during the period. However, three things happened that improved the prospects for secularists in the second half of the century: the development of German higher criticism of the Bible, the Civil War, and the publication of Darwin's theory. Mark Noll has argued that of the three, the Civil War may have been the one most damaging to the public dominance of Christianity because of the claims to Christian fidelity made by two parties on opposing sides of the fundamental spiritual, ideological, and moral issue of slavery. But all three developments took a heavy toll on elites.

Darwinism and higher criticism contributed to the fundamentalist-modernist controversy, which resulted in the establishment of two main camps of Protestants in America: the mainline and the fundamentalists. The word *fundamentalist* tends to evoke images of uneducated rubes for many people, but the early fundamentalists were often well-educated Christians determined to defend the core doctrines of the faith. (In our culture, *fundamentalist* has become a word that describes an unthinking person. Alvin Plantinga has humorously noted that *fundamentalist* is often used simply to mean the SOB "to the right" of oneself and one's "enlightened friends.")[4] The fundamentalists lost the battle for the mainline Protestant denominations. Between that loss and their apparent humiliation in the Scopes trial in Tennessee, fundamentalists appeared to retreat far into the margins of American life, so far that they were somewhat forgotten.

During the same period of decades in the late nineteenth and early twentieth century, secularists made serious inroads into American colleges and universities. Though higher education in America had once been almost exclusively Christian, the aforementioned trifecta of cultural shocks, plus the simple desire of some elites for more secular sensibilities in the academy, led to big changes. Contrary to the claims of secularization theorists, the transition was not simply a natural one. Christian Smith's book *The Secular Revolution* documents the determined way in which secularists worked to transform many sectors of American life to suit their preferences. George Marsden's *The Soul of the American University* features an especially telling account of the way officers of a Carnegie fund offered pension funds for professors to those schools that were willing to sever their church ties. Within the first four years of the fund's existence, twenty schools dropped their sponsoring denominations. Marsden introduced his book with the story of William F. Buckley Jr.'s publication of *God and Man at Yale* in 1951 and the subsequent fallout. One of Buckley's most bombastic assertions was that Yale University no longer cared about its Christian roots. What interested Marsden was that Yale *strenuously denied* Buckley's claims. One can see how far we have come by attempting to transplant that controversy to the current day. It would be impossible. Yale is now entirely immune to caring about such a claim and has been for decades. (A fellow professor with an Ivy League pedigree read these remarks and insisted that Yale is

---

4. Alvin Plantinga, *Warranted Christian Belief* (New York: Oxford University Press, 2000), 244–45.

not only immune to caring about such a claim, but that they would vigorously deny any link to the Christian faith today!)

Meanwhile, the losers of the fundamentalist-modernist controversy were busy heeding the call "be ye separate." Joel Carpenter has documented how they constructed a series of parallel institutions. The people we think of as evangelicals today began as the neo-evangelicals who arose from the fundamentalist movement. Their special concern was to reengage with the culture and not only to fight the old doctrinal battles again. Rather than just take on the mainline churches, they hoped to bring the Christian worldview to bear on many areas of life such as politics, the arts, and education. Carl F. H. Henry was one of the early contributors to this effort with his *The Uneasy Conscience of Modern Fundamentalism*. The visible manifestation of the neo-evangelicals' presence was the rising fame of Billy Graham, who was a key figure in many evangelical institutions as well as a phenomenally successful revivalist preacher. While the mainline church was losing steam due to the enervating effect of its many concessions to modernity, evangelicals were rising.

Evangelicals would not begin to make a more obvious impact outside of the church until the 1970s and the period after *Roe v. Wade*. There are a couple of reasons why this occurred that are worth reciting here. One is that many evangelicals wanted to escape the isolation of fundamentalism, but still viewed politics suspiciously. Another is that evangelicals (and certainly fundamentalists) had little interest in making common cause against secularists with their most obvious ally, Roman Catholics. For quite some time, evangelicals listed secularism, Communism, and Romanism as evils they needed to resist. But after *Roe*, voices such as Francis Schaeffer urged both political engagement and co-belligerence with Catholics against secular materialism. One could argue that *Roe* bridged the gap between evangelicals and Catholics in a way that intentional efforts at ecumenism never could.

To secular American elites, who were by this time firmly in control of the institutions such as the media and universities that legitimate knowledge and help create the range of acceptable consensus, the mid-1970s were a nasty shock due to the sudden reemergence of a public Christianity that was willing to openly confront the dominant philosophies. Many secularists had believed that such people disappeared after the Scopes trial and would not return. Chuck Colson, previously known as Richard Nixon's ax man, converted to Christianity and penned the best seller *Born Again*. Jimmy Carter, a born-again believer, was elected president and was even supported by Pat Robertson. Magazines like *Time* and *Newsweek* began to rediscover the various stripes of conservative Christians. The phenomenon would eventually result in the Moral Majority, the Christian Coalition, James Dobson's Focus on the Family, and a network of institutions, publications, and broadcasts that was more extensive than probably anyone realized. This phenomenon would also eventually see the expansion of the Christian voice in academic circles with publications such as *First Things* and *Books and Culture*, as well as renewed Christian seriousness at Baylor University, which has become a Carnegie research university with a billion-dollar endowment. With all this activity, Christians (certainly conservative Christians) are arguably engaging in the contest of worldviews with much more power and effect than they did during much of the twentieth century.

The response of secularists has been twofold. First, they have continued the strategy of removing the Judeo-Christian symbols and special allowances from the facilities and practices of public entities. This part of the program is at least understandable and partially justifiable because of the increasing pluralism of contemporary America. We can no longer take our homogeneity for granted. However, one might make a strong case that symbols and messages such as the Ten Commandments, the cross, and nativity scenes enjoy a genetic connection to American culture and deserve some deference. Nations have cultures and traditions. They do not simply spring forth like Athena full-grown from Zeus' troubled brow. It is perhaps too infrequently considered that washing away such vestiges may burden many citizens as much or more than it creates a greater sense of freedom or belonging for others. In the case of religious symbols and the apparatus of the state, we might be better off, as Steven Smith has suggested, not to draw rigid lines, and to look more closely at what amount of real harm is caused rather than abstract principles.[5]

---

5. Steven D. Smith, *The Disenchantment of Secular Discourse* (Cambridge, MA: Harvard University Press, 2010).

Second, secularists have, especially since the seemingly sudden appearance of the religious Right, appealed to an ideal of secular reason. The idea seems to be that as long as a person makes an argument for a particular value-laden position without citing any religious authority or reflection in support of it, then the position is reasonable. If the public contestant makes an argument by relying on a religious revelation or tradition for all or part of his support, then that is considered very poor form and not virtuous.

There are three problems with this type of secular opposition to religious politicking. The first is that this kind of secular opposition penalizes the citizen who is willing to state the foundation for his values, but it does not penalize the one who neglects to state such a foundation. How much of political discourse relies on quasi-religious assertions of what is right or wrong? Why should a person who puts all his cards on the table about his motivation or about what he finds compelling be penalized by some artificial rules about political discourse?

The second problem is that an insistence on the virtue of secular political discourse over more religious argumentation mistakes a common feature of politics for a special imposition of religion in the public square. The fact is that politics is about winning and losing on questions of what human beings must do in the part of their lives that is collective and obligatory. What is most objectionable about the situation is not whether an opponent has a religious reason for being pro-life or pro-environment or anti–free market, or what have you. What is hard to swallow is the imposition of one group's values on another group through politics. This is an unavoidable feature of the activity. For this reason, Milton Friedman has argued for the superiority of non-political solutions over political ones. The political solutions, according to Friedman, strain social cohesion.[6]

The third problem with the case for secular political discourse is that its advocates have been exceptionally selective in their outrage. Stephen Carter has noted this dynamic in *The Culture of Disbelief*. Religious calls for progressive positions on civil rights, the Cold War, and the Vietnam War met with great enthusiasm from the media and

6. Milton Friedman, *Capitalism and Freedom: 40th Anniversary Edition* (Chicago: University of Chicago Press, 2002).

government elites. At that time, there were no top academic voices talking about the importance of offering only public reasons (read: secular reasons) that any person could reasonably accept.

When religious liberals involve themselves in politics, they are "speaking truth to power" and "filling a prophetic role" in public affairs. When religious conservatives involve themselves in politics, however, they are pilloried as potential theocrats and oppressors who want to return us to the Middle Ages (or, more polemically, the *Dark* Ages), and this despite the fact that on the issue they care most about they are certainly speaking prophetically. That issue is abortion. Carter believes the Supreme Court's decision in *Roe v. Wade* and its subsequent mass mobilization of religious conservatives is the watershed event that changed perception of the desirability of the religious voice in the public square. It is an interesting coincidence of history that political philosophers began to argue for the exclusion of religious reason from public discourse during the same period when abortion legalization debates began to occupy the consciences of Americans before and after *Roe*. Religious appeals were fine for the civil rights movement and for anti-Vietnam protesters. There is no such equal opportunity for pro-lifers.

The change in the nature of religious speakers in politics was obvious. Carter writes: "And so the public rhetoric of religion, which from the time of the abolitionist movement through the era of the 'social gospel' and well into the 1960s and early 1970s had largely been the property of liberalism, was all at once—and quite thunderously, too—the special province of people fighting for a cause that the left considered an affront."[7] With that sea change in the composition of religious speakers in the public square came the corresponding alteration in how such speakers were viewed and treated. Consider how easily pro-life advocates and demonstrators might have been viewed as latter-day civil rights marchers, and yet to this day they are not viewed that way by anyone except their coreligionists. In point of fact, their right to protest has been restricted and confined in a way that would have been decried with great emotion had the same been done to civil rights protesters of the 1960s. It is almost

---

7. Stephen Carter, *The Culture of Disbelief: How American Law and Politics Trivialize Religious Devotion* (New York: Basic Books, 1993), 58.

unimaginable that protesters staging sit-ins at segregated businesses and institutions in the 1960s would have been hit with RICO (Racketeering Influenced Corrupt Organizations) lawsuits (backed by the full force of the federal government) originally designed to deal with organized crime. Yet several pro-life protesters suffered that fate. When religious conservatives speak truth to power, they do not seem to earn the esteem of either the society or the secular state the way some of their liberal predecessors did.

Carter's main point is that social elites seek to marginalize the religious influence whenever it expresses a worldview with which they disagree. Thus, when the left-wing nuclear freeze group or poverty rights group speaks in frankly religious terms, it is everything secular liberals find good and ennobling about religion. They feel, for a moment, that they could live with this kind of faith in politics. But when the right-wing abortion protester or advocate of traditional marriage speaks, it is seen as a frightening threat of theocracy.

Just to underline the point, there are a couple of strong examples that can be offered. First, at the very same time secularists assailed Judge Roy Moore in Alabama for his Ten Commandments' display, a liberal law professor named Susan Pace Hamill convinced Alabama's Reaganite governor to crusade for significant reform of the tax code in order to make it more amenable to the ethics of Jesus Christ. The proposed method of achieving that goal was to make the state's tax code more progressive. While Moore's symbolic stand drew massive attention and legal opposition, the reform of the tax code (something that is at the heart of governmental operations) according to Judeo-Christian ethics drew virtually no protest from secularists.

Second, and of critical importance, is Martin Luther King Jr.'s "Letter from Birmingham Jail." In that letter, King brilliantly spoke of Christian ethical themes as a justification for battling segregation. He referenced biblical stories and thinkers such as Augustine and Aquinas. While it is true that the letter was written to white pastors, and so was not explicitly political, it has become a classic of American political rhetoric. It stands as a nice counterpoint to another letter written to pastors, Thomas Jefferson's response to the Danbury Baptists in which he penned the phrase "a wall of separation between church and state," upon which many jurists have relied. The church, King wrote, should be a thermostat, not a thermometer.

It should act to affect the broader culture, not simply offer a reading of where the culture stands.

I have found that defenders of secularism tend to resist applying their usual policy to King's letter, but I do not think principle really permits something like a King exception. We either permit religious speech and expression to enter the arena on a par with everything else or we uphold an artificial construct of proper secular discourse. The right policy is just what the legal scholar Sanford Levinson suggested when he considered this matter. The natural and proper limit on discourse, he wrote, is persuasion.[8] If a religious person offers arguments and reasons that resonate (regardless of the religiosity of the arguments), then he may succeed in convincing others. If he does not offer reasons and arguments that resonate, then he will likely fail.

I would like to point out one more blind spot that I think secularists have. There is a strong tendency among secularists to treat religion as a general phenomenon that can be considered as a single piece. Sophisticated observers should realize that there is little sense in treating religion as a commodity. In the TV show *The Simpsons*, Ned Flanders' beleaguered pastor once counseled him to consider another religion because "they're all basically the same," but the truth is quite different. The western package of rights and freedoms has a special relationship to Christianity, for example, that it does not necessarily share with Islam. Christianity is rising in the southern nations and may be blooming in China. I am confident that the effect will ultimately be different in those places than it would be if Islam were to dominate.

Therefore, I cannot understand why some of the more ardent secularists, such as Brian Leiter of the University of Chicago, insist on referring to conservative Christians with labels such as "The Texas Taliban," or why so many American liberals seems to fear evangelicals as much or more than they do Islamic extremists. It may be true that a rose is a rose is a rose, but we cannot speak similarly about religions.

---

8. Sanford Levinson, "Religious Language and the Public Square," review of *Love and Power: The Role of Religion and Morality in American Politics*, by Michael J. Perry, *Harvard Law Review* 105 (June 1992): 2077.

Finally, I would like to circle back to the theme of secularization in society. When people hear that I have written a book titled *The End of Secularism*, they are usually puzzled. Have I not seen the surveys that show that more people today identify their religion as "none" than in previous years? Do I not see the apparent popularity of the new atheists?

The first thing I say is that I do not predict the end of secularism. I simply argue that it holds little promise as a public philosophy for pluralistic societies. But more important, I think, is to realize that if Peter Berger and others are right about pluralism rather than secularism being the outcome of modernity, then one would expect to see secularists have their moment in the sun when they begin to realize the full scope of their demographic. That is happening now. America, for example, is now much less of a melting pot where people are expected to fit in and more like a salad bowl where the ingredients maintain their distinctiveness. Secularists and atheists feel that they can much more easily express themselves openly. They are finding one another and feel emboldened. The same thing happened with conservatives after Barry Goldwater, Ronald Reagan, and Rush Limbaugh, and with evangelical Christians after Billy Graham, Francis Schaeffer, and James Dobson.

The clash of orthodoxies, as Robert George has labeled it, is on. The main thing that is missing as we set up the arena for an open and honest exchange is for the secularists to realize that they are participants in that clash rather than the referees.

Five

SECULAR STATISM
AND THE TRAVAIL
OF RELIGIOUS LIBERTY

S ecular statism presents a serious threat to religious liberty and rights of conscience. Barring a substantial rollback in the size of government, the best response to secular statism is a renewed cultural emphasis on religious liberty and toleration as necessary components of freedom in a highly pluralistic society.

What is secular statism? One might begin by defining both parts. Secular, in this case, refers to a public philosophy that emphasizes the privatization of religion. Statism is the belief that most of our social problems can best be addressed through government action of some kind. Statists, therefore, regularly seek to expand the powers of government in order to achieve a perceived greater good. Secular statists pursue a vision of a government (often heedless of religion), which addresses itself comprehensively to the needs of citizens.

There are a number of possible objections to secular statism. Many of these objections relate to prudential matters such as the economic performance of secular statist governments versus the results garnered by freer alternatives. The goal of the present chapter, however, is to demonstrate the danger that secular statism poses to liberty of religion and conscience. These are the liberties many of us would consider the most important.

In order to illustrate the danger of secular statism, I will add two recent case studies to the philosophical discussion. The first is the Department of Health and Human Services mandate (or HHS mandate) that requires virtually all employers, both private and nonprofit, to provide contraceptive and abortifacient products as part of their insurance plans. The second is the recent controversy over Chick-fil-A senior executive Dan Cathy's remarks in which he expressed his opposition to gay marriage.

We may begin by thinking about the nature of the state. For a long time, institutional power, both religious and political, tended to be concentrated together. To be born into a community would be to simultaneously have civil and cultic membership.

The life of Jesus and the subsequent rise of the Christian church caused a tremendous disruption in this pattern. Thanks to the size of their empire, the Romans had learned how to deal with religious pluralism. They simply allowed different peoples to have their gods as long as the people were willing to worship the emperor. Generally speaking, people accepted those conditions. One of the distinguishing factors of the early Christian church is that it would not worship the emperor. The Christians would bow the knee only to their lord, Jesus Christ, who had been raised from the dead. The apostle Paul had the audacity to speak of the resurrection even in the debating society of the men of Athens (Acts 17:16–34).

The impact of Jesus, as Rousseau would later complain, was to introduce the problem of two masters. No longer did political and religious power necessarily travel together. Hobbes and Rousseau thought political communities should not have two masters. Better, they thought, to again unite the two powers under one head, as was the case with Hobbes' Leviathan. Rousseau had good intentions when he wrote a philosophy fit for totalitarians. He is remembered for lamenting that man is born free, but is found everywhere in chains. Less often do we hear another thought of his that relates to freedom, which is that if a citizen disagrees with the general will of the nation, then he or she *must be forced to be free.* For Rousseau, freedom was more about the right to participate in democratic deliberation than it was about protecting a semi-inviolable sphere of action and conscience from the ambitions of the state or other powers. The HHS mandate is an example of exactly such a sentiment. As long as one is in the majority, then one feels free to impose.

Like Rousseau, John Locke reasoned about the nature of the social contract. But, unlike Rousseau, he did not conclude that freedom consists in being forced to follow the general will. Instead, he said that government exists to make us more truly free, free in a sense that we can actually understand and support. In a state of nature, there is still a natural law of right and wrong that exists, but the ability of human beings to enforce it is in question. It is possible, for example, that a thief could overwhelm a person and take his or her goods. While natural law identifies the offense and a person's right to punish the thief and recover the stolen goods, that same law hardly provides a person with a strong mechanism to do so. When we have a low probability of achieving that result without a government, we lose little by creating a state to protect us from the violent or dishonest acts of others. In other words, we gain freedom by empowering a state to punish criminal acts. Rather than being *forced to be free*, the government will *use force to protect freedom*.

The goal of government, on this view, is to protect freedom, not to diminish it. Such a government should not infringe on the freedoms of religion and conscience. These are the freedoms we should be *least* likely to bargain away because they are the most important. The state should not enact laws and regulations that create a situation in which individuals become opponents of the entity that is designed to protect them in the exercise of their freedom. This makes people enemies of the state when they have done nothing by way of force or fraud that should make the state see them as enemies.

There are certain things that belong to the state and other things that do not. One of Locke's great insights is that the earthly state is an instrument, not some kind of great end. It is a temporal tool designed to solve a simple problem, which is the problem of restraining evil so as to protect freedom. The state is designed to serve persons. Persons are not designed to serve the state. The great French Catholic scholar Jacques Maritain said it best: The state is made for man, not man for the state.[1] It is a very dangerous thing to invert that

---

1. Jacques Maritain, *Man and the State* (Washington, DC: Catholic University of America Press, 1998), 13.

relationship. The best example of the inverse view is a nightmare of a little nation that we know as North Korea.

The United States traditionally has been one of the nations that most clearly understands the proper role of the government. This nation has welcomed the existence and development of many institutions of civil society (the church included) that perform tasks that need not belong to the state. What Rousseau missed that Locke understood is that when government attempts to rule over too much of life, then there are too many areas in which disagreement can only be settled with the exercise of coercive power, which includes things such as civil penalties and imprisonment. A nation should only resort to those harsh tools when the stakes are very high. Why would we subject more things to that official (and ultimately punitive) sphere than we must?

This type of reasoning is evident in Thomas Paine's influential revolutionary tract *Common Sense*. Paine reasoned that human beings living together in community have resort to two ways of getting around their atomistic aloneness and the reduced usefulness that comes from that aloneness. He calls these two ways society and government. Society is what happens, for example, when a man realizes that he can either spend years trying to accomplish his individual purposes alone or he can enter into voluntary cooperation with a number of others to accomplish both his purposes and theirs in a much shorter period. Generally speaking, this voluntary sphere that Paine calls society is by far the best option for living in community. However, Paine recognizes that some individuals will do wrong and cause injury or place unjust burdens upon their neighbors. These sorts of actions create the need for the second sphere, which Paine calls government. It is the responsibility of government to employ coercion. This coercive method of government should be used only when truly necessary since the government has a tendency to grow and swallow large areas of human endeavor.

If human beings make use of the voluntary society sphere, then they will have strong institutions other than the government. The presence of these other strong institutions actually improves the prospects for freedom. The family, the church, the private school, charitable organizations—all of which are institutions in the voluntary society sector rather than in the government—represent alternative allegiances for people. Alternative allegiances help to limit the power of the state and to curb its ambitions. A totalitarian state prefers to have only two entities in society, namely the individual and the state. In that situation, the state's vision will always be supreme. No totalitarian or authoritarian state will permit the problem of the two masters. Perhaps we should reconsider whether the problem of the two masters is a problem after all.

The United States has been a great experiment in having many different sources of authority. It has had local, state, and federal governments. Its federal structure contains different branches of the government that alternately contend and cooperate with one another. The classic question in politics has been, who has the power? One of the great American contributions has been not only to divide the power between different entities and persons, but also to ask a still more fundamental question, how much power? Thus, the United States has been a great example of limited government. There are simply some things that do not belong to the government. The power of American government is really less inherent and comprehensive than it is delegated and selective.

The idea of limited and delegated government powers relates nicely to the concept of the separation of church and state. Too often the separation of church and state is thought of as simply a curb on the ambitions of the church to wield political powers and to fill its coffers with taxes rather than tithes. That is the secularist reading of separation. A better reading of separation is to connect it to the idea of limited government. The church is separate from the state because the state does not own people's souls. It should have no right to coerce them in that regard. With the separation of church and state, it is true that no taxes will fill offering plates. But separation also means that no civil authorities will run seminaries or decide who may fill a pulpit or what may be preached. The separation of church and state may be properly understood as a limitation on the ambitions of the state.

The partisans of secular statism, some of whom work through the institutions of the United States government, are making arguments and taking actions that are designed to embrace a more Rousseauian understanding with regard to the nature of the state and any religion in the state. These arguments and actions cut against the grain of the idea of limited government.

With that preface in place, two recent controversies are worth examining in relation to the problem of secular statism. They are the HHS mandate and the Chick-fil-A gay marriage controversy.

The HHS mandate requires employers to provide insurance coverage for their employees that include abortifacient and contraceptive products and services. It effectively contains no exemption for religious institutions such as universities, charities, and hospitals that might find it difficult to comply for reasons of faith and conscience.

The mandate handed down by means of an essentially undemocratic regulatory process by the government's Department of Health and Human Services is a direct incursion by the state upon the church's ability to participate in the broader society. The kind of government that is comfortable writing and enforcing this type of regulation is one that sees itself as possessing comprehensive authority. In essence, the state and its officials are saying that its conception of what is good for human beings is superior to the church's view and it will be made mandatory (even for church institutions) regardless of the church's objections. The choice of mechanism—simply grabbing either church employers or their insurers and saying, "You, pay for this!"—is particularly destructive because the state forces others to bear both the cost and the moral weight of its policy rather than simply funding on its own what it claims is good. There would be no lawsuit if the federal government simply provided contraceptives and abortifacients to female citizens. Instead, the government insists that people who object must themselves pay for these items. It should be evident how violent this policy is toward the consciences of those who pay for and run religious organizations.

Whether its members realize it or not, the Obama administration did its work directly under Rousseau's canopy. It would have been simple to either provide the required products and services directly through the government or to insert a provision into the mandate that accommodated objections based on faith and conscience. Employees working for religious employers hardly represent a large portion of the labor force. But the accommodation has not been made in any meaningful sense. One has the feeling that the accommodation has not been made because the regulators are working from their own view of principle. They are saying, with Rousseau, that what they see as civil and theological intolerance cannot stand. The Christian church finds itself at odds with the metaphysics of the United States government.

Those who prefer a larger government and believe it is the primary provider for the good of people tend to think the mandate is a just measure. But I have discovered that people who hold this view are able to see the problem with the mandate when I change the fact situation to one with which they are more sympathetic. For example, let us imagine a Quaker college with a core conviction regarding pacifism. What if the government were to insist that such a college host an ROTC unit on campus? Given these facts, should the Quaker college simply buckle under the pressure, ignore its core beliefs, and do what the government says? Put that way, supporters of the mandate may suddenly understand the problem with the situation that the government is putting the church in. If the issue is pacifism rather than sex or reproduction, then the matter of conscientious and spiritual objection becomes more clear. We can be blind to important principles when our particular ox is not being gored.

Though the thrust of the argument here deals with religious liberty, we should perhaps not fail to notice that maybe the issue is simply liberty itself. In 2009, then Congressman Bart Stupak and a group of pro-life Democrats held up passage of the president's health care bill because of their concerns about taxpayer money being spent on abortions and because of a desire to make sure that conscience would be protected. After the president signed an executive order aimed at alleviating their concerns, Stupak's group provided the winning margin in the House of Representatives. Stupak and his group of fellow congressmen had attempted to protect religious liberty and rights of conscience in the massive piece of legislation, but all that is a faint memory now. The warning that becomes clear in the way the Affordable Care Act led to the HHS mandate is that if we as a nation insist on continuing to expand the power we give to the government, then we should not be shocked and dismayed when we see fundamental rights and freedoms, such as religious liberty, eroded. We must be very careful and very sure of what we are doing when we seek to expand the power of the state. A laudable attempt to provide health care coverage for more Americans has ended up posing a threat to citizens and institutions that have substantive disagreements with the HHS mandate that are based on religion and conscience.

If it is true that something like the HHS mandate might eventually have the effect of forcing the church to abandon its efforts in running schools, universities, hospitals, and social services, then a pragmatic person may well rethink the mandate for fear of losing all the good that religious institutions do. But for people of a certain ideological stripe, losing the good of religious institutions may well be acceptable as a way of resolving the two masters issue.

While the HHS mandate is problematic for various religionists and their institutions, there is a second controversy with the potential to cause much larger problems. This second case highlights the question of whether the issue of gay marriage will end up dissolving religious liberty because of the clash it initiates between two prime American values: liberty and equality.

In 2012, Dan Cathy—son of Truett Cathy, who founded the much-loved Chick-fil-A restaurants—answered honestly and affirmatively when asked whether he opposes gay marriage. "Guilty as charged," he replied. Although there was an immediate reaction against Chick-fil-A, comments by the mayors of both Boston and Chicago to the effect that Chick-fil-A might be barred from operating in their cities were the match that lit the fuse of counterprotest. Mike Huckabee, the former governor of Arkansas, seized the moment to make a call for a show of support for the Cathy family. At the grassroots level, customers flooded into the restaurants to provide a measure of protection for the company. Publicly, the message was clear: There were many Americans who did not want to see Chick-fil-A suffer for the sincere statement of values offered by Dan Cathy. The demonstration of solidarity with Chick-fil-A offered the company shelter and perhaps led the company's critics to wonder whether they had overplayed their hand.

The reaction of secular statists toward Chick-fil-A suggests that Cathy's opinion is not one that will be tolerated for long. Cathy's opponents believe his opinion is not merely deserving of their disagreement, but, what is more, that it should be viewed as a clear evil, which should be extinguished by political means if necessary.

Some will say that the critics of Chick-fil-A were correct in their moral intuitions because the company stands in the same place as segregationists of the Old South. This type of argument must be faced in order to successfully maintain the religious liberty side of the argument. If the conclusion of American law and policy is that resistance to gay marriage is essentially equivalent to a preference for slavery or segregation, then religious liberty will serve as no shield at all because there is no respect for those invidious points of view. Thus, it is necessary to respond to the assertion that opposition to gay marriage is morally equivalent to support for slavery or segregation or both. Throughout the following discussion, keep in mind that the goal is not to convince the reader of the case against gay marriage. Rather, the goal is to convince the reader that opposition to gay marriage is neither invidious nor unworthy of respect.

Rather than beginning with the idea of traditional marriage as a structure that opposes something that is now viewed as a goal in society, we should instead see traditional male-female marriage as the tremendously good institution that it is and has been. It is an answer to the problem of human loneliness and incompleteness. This relationship is also fruitful. While marriage gives the man and the woman a companion in the form of each other, it also leads to the reproduction of human beings such that we have families, clans, villages, towns, cities, and, ultimately, states and nations. Interestingly, Aristotle did not identify the individual as the basis of political society. Instead, he viewed the family (based on the man and the woman) as the fundamental unit. It is easy to see why. Without male-female procreation, society literally has no future. Traditional marriage sets forth an ideal in which the man stays with and supports the woman both while she is most vulnerable during pregnancy and later while they both care for children. Marriage recognizes that the man and woman are both necessary to the creation of the child as well as the process of child rearing. It is important to note that marriage follows biology. Marriages rose out of the physical and reproductive complementarity of men and women. Without sex and reproduction, there would likely be no such thing as marriage. It is, therefore, no surprise that many theists view marriage as God's design.

It is also the case that we have known for several years now that as a group children who grow up in traditional, two-parent homes do better than their peers from single-parent or divorced homes in virtually any social statistic one might wish to name. There is inadequate evidence with regard to children in homes with same-sex parents, though it is interesting to note that the sociologist Mark Regnerus performed such a study and was made the subject of an investigation by the University of Texas for his efforts.

Given the facts of biology and the practical realities of raising children, male-female marriage makes a tremendous amount of sense. So, with both reason and revelation in mind, many Christians and others have insisted that marriage should continue to have its traditional shape. This is not some bizarre, novel, aggressive position. In fact, this was the position of President Obama until a few years ago.

To illustrate the historical posture toward traditional marriage, compare the historical record on marriage to the historical record of slavery. While the history of slavery is as long as human history itself, there is evidence that it was something of a live issue, always something that a number of people considered to be wrong. Aristotle included a discussion of slavery in his *Politics*. It is clear that there were people who thought it was wrong and who gave reasons against the practice. To my knowledge, there is no such record of advocacy for gay marriage in antiquity.

Where gay marriage has prevailed in courts, jurists have treated the case against gay marriage as though it were completely irrational. But is it really irrational? Remember that one may find the opposition to gay marriage rational and still disagree with the opposition. To affirm that the opposition is rational merely means that one can see how the opponents justify their position and that their reasoning does not resemble the words of a person who thinks the moon is made of green cheese. It is important to note, though, that arguments advanced in favor of something such as race-based segregation do take on the quality of "green cheese" assertions. They partake substantially of irrationality.

Given this background, it would seem that to insist that members and institutions of the Christian church should suddenly reject the essentially unanimous testimony of history (and Christian practice and scripture) regarding marriage demands too much. Opposition to gay marriage does not appear to be similar to favoring slavery or segregation of the races. The impact of gay marriage on society is something worth considering, but so is the impact of gay marriage on religious liberty. If it becomes normal to view opposition to gay marriage as basically akin to racism, then tremendous damage will be done to Christian institutions. Secular statism will roll right over them. They will lose the right to participate in the public life of our country.

One precedent to consider is the situation of Bob Jones University, which lost its tax exemption because it forbade interracial dating. Although we affirm that the university's policy was racist and ugly, will it similarly come to pass that Wheaton College or Franciscan University of Steubenville will lose their tax-exempt status because they refuse to recognize gay marriage or hire those who have same-sex spouses? Will the writers of laws and regulations try to prevent students at such places from obtaining federal loans or other aid on the basis of some discrimination perceived as unjust? Many will argue that such action against Christian colleges and institutions is exactly the kind of action that should be taken. But if it is true that opposition to gay marriage is different in kind rather than in degree from various race-based discriminations, as I have argued above, then the ability of Christian and other religious institutions to participate in public life should not be threatened.

We need a new lens through which to view some of our public values and their relation to religious liberty because both the religious pluralism and values pluralism of the United States continue to grow. The cultural consensus, as Francis Schaeffer used to call it, is vanishing. We will need some new view of toleration if we are to avoid using political power to resolve a series of controversies related to conscience. Rights such as religious liberty have traditionally been protected by constitutions for exactly the reason that they are highly vulnerable to democratic intrusion by majorities. Without some renewal of appreciation for that fundamental dynamic in our law, we will see both incursions and corresponding resentment increase. A refusal to tolerate differences rooted in conscience and religion makes enemies of people relative to the state. The error is an unforced one. We should hope that future policymakers and jurists work by clear light in this regard.

Six

SECULARISM AND SOCIALISM: TWO FORMS OF SOCIAL LEVELING

S ocial leveling, as I noted in chapter 4, is something that we typically associate with the destruction of material differences between human beings. It is the socialist dream of a classless society in which distinctions, usually the result of economic variation, are made irrelevant. The state, empowered by the political action of the masses (or at least a group claiming to speak for the masses), works to gain control of the wealth and property of a society and then to redistribute it in such a way as to make people equal. It should be obvious that this type of action vastly increases the power of the state because it becomes the effective owner of all property.

Although socialism aims to wipe out material inequality, it may merely present a new opportunity for sin. In *The Federalist* #10, James Madison noted that investing human beings with substantial democratic rights will not make for equality of circumstance. Citizens have different talents, abilities, and levels of energy. Those differences will tell. Madison hoped to deal with the differences by opposing the energy of factions against each other. The levelers naïvely assumed that they could make men so equal as to make their interests the same and to tie their destinies firmly together. But a new elite will assert itself, just as it has in every nation with a communist revolution. The difference is that instead of the productive computer genius earning the luxuries of life, it goes to a gifted political functionary or some other obedient person. Forced economic leveling performed by the state is intended to erase the sin of greed, but it turns out that someone has to make the sacrifice of living at the mountain retreat with the on-call sushi chef!

Although there have been Christian socialists, socialism has primarily been the province of secularists. I suspect that is because while it easy to understand why Christians could endorse a voluntary sharing of all property, it is harder to see why they would endorse the kind of *involuntary* sharing that a more brusque person might refer to as coercive confiscation legitimized by government power. Augustine shared this perspective when he pictured some governments as bands of robbers with official uniforms of state.

Political leftists often criticized Ronald Reagan for his great willingness to help individual persons who asked for his aid while he was simultaneously opposed to erecting great structural plans of income redistribution or expansion of the welfare state. He did this because he was interested in the virtue of one person helping another. Interestingly, Aristotle held the same position. He decried socialism because it would replace the beauty of voluntary giving with a state-imposed sameness of means. Reagan knew it was right for him to sign a check and send it to a person in need. He did not presume to do that on someone else's behalf by confiscating their funds.

The logic of social leveling can be extended in many directions. Plato applied it to property and to family. Members of his imaginary guardian class were to have common wives, common children, and common property. Making sure that all of them had basically the same things was designed to create great empathy and cooperation. Thus, Plato imagined that when one felt pain, all would feel pain and move to heal it. Conversely, when one felt pleasure, all would enjoy it.

There is a serious problem with this line of thinking, and it has to do with human nature. As we have seen, Aristotle pointed out that the man with a thousand sons really has no son. The man with one son is almost surely willing to give his life for him. The preference for the particular over the general has broader application. A field that is owned by everyone is unlikely to be plowed. But a field owned by one man is likely to be as productive as he can make it. Starvation was a perennial problem in China until the communists began to yield this point.

There is another reason why Christians are unlikely to embrace social leveling. The logic of social leveling applies to more than property. The relationship between socialism and secularism proceeds from the desire to erase differences and emphasize equality. Socialism recommends a course of action designed to erase the economic distinctions between human beings by taking individual choices about property out of people's hands. Secularism operates in such a way as to diminish the impact of religious differences between people (and then cause them to disappear entirely) by making religion irrelevant to the life of the community. This action of secularism, so similar to socialism, is why I refer to it as a type of social leveling.

There is an intuitive appeal to social leveling. Equality is an important value. Our political system must take it into account. But there are many hazards involved in systemic applications of the principle. Applying social leveling to property or economic achievement takes no cognizance of merit or virtue and thus diminishes the value of both property and economic achievement. Social leveling directed toward religious matters trivializes the search for truth. Indeed, it implicitly denies the possibility of religious truth. All religious propositions are treated as utterly unprovable revelations that are fit primarily for the credulous. This presents a special problem for Christians who believe that their faith is actually true and that there is historical evidence available to support it. One should not be surprised that secularists view Christianity as a psychological crutch. They think Christians adopt their faith for primarily emotional reasons. Yet, the power of Paul at the Areopagus, or of people like C. S. Lewis or Francis Schaeffer in the modern era, comes from pulling the crucifixion and resurrection into the public square and saying, "This really happened. And if it did, don't you think it is important that we figure out what it means?"

Social leveling in the form of secularism does faithfully treat all religions the same. All religions become equally private and equally segregated from the life of the community. Secularists, of course, hope that religion will eventually fade away as human beings embrace their equality with each other. The empirical evidence, however, tends to run in a direction contrary to that secularist hope. If there is any equality among human beings, it is equality before God who has placed his image upon all of us.

I have argued that social leveling achieves a wrong result in the sense that, in the form of socialism, it ignores things like merit and virtue, and, in the form of secularism, it ignores truth. That alone is good reason to oppose it, but there is a bigger problem than that. The social leveling that is achieved by socialism and secularism can only be engineered by one entity in a society. That entity is the state. Thus, the state will become the effective owner of all property and the state will determine what manifestations of religion (if any) are acceptable to itself.

If we empower the state to this degree, then the state effectively dictates reality and tends to move in the direction of totalitarianism. It is notable that the Marxist dream of human brotherhood rooted in universal equality stalled out repeatedly at the dictatorship stage without any prospect of moving forward to the "withering away of the state" that Marx had predicted. This tendency toward dictatorship among nations opting for radical brotherhood seems to confirm the American founders' view of the human being and to disconfirm Marx's view. In other words, the suspicion of power fostered by a Christian awareness of human sinfulness is a more realistic approach. That suspicion led the American founders to build a system that makes dictatorship, or the functional equivalent, extraordinarily difficult to achieve.

In a system where the state has the power to engage in social leveling, institutions that would compete with the state for influence must be minimized. So, for example, the school system is used to transmit values to children. Those values will be values dictated by the state. In this way, the influence of other institutions in the society, such as families and churches, can be blunted in favor of the state's chosen message transmitter. Americans are fortunate to live in a society where the education function is not monopolized by the state. It is, however, highly subsidized, and alternative choices involve what amounts to a financial penalty.

In the United States, there is still a healthy debate about what ought to be taught in schools, and there is freedom to withdraw from the schools. But in a social leveler state, no such choice exists.

Imagine how difficult it would be to instill ideas and information in a child when those ideas and information are in conflict with the message of the state institution that dominates the child's day. In that child's life, everything that is officially evaluated says that what the family or church believes is unimportant.

The totalitarian logic includes only two classes of actors in the society: the state and the individual. The individual is expected to serve the purposes of the state. This dynamic also partially explains the enthusiasm of social levelers for secularism. If the church is vital within the society, then it offers an independent voice that can compete with the state for the hearts and minds of the people. The history of Poland offers an extraordinary example. Poland resisted communism more effectively than many other nations because its Catholic church staunchly stood up for its rights and encouraged the people to see themselves as human beings who should be free. During that time, Karol Wojtyła, the man who would become Pope John Paul II, encouraged young people to accompany him on wilderness hikes and canoeing trips to help them develop space for freedom from the state. His underlying message: The state is not the supreme reality. There is more to life than the state. A church, independent of the state, enhances freedom. Jacques Maritain nicely captured this role of the church when he wrote: "In the course of twenty centuries, by preaching the Gospel to the nations and by standing up to the flesh and blood powers in order to defend against them the liberties of spirit, the Church has taught men freedom."[1]

The twentieth century was the century par excellence for social leveling. At no other time in history was there so much energy behind experiments in government on a massive scale. It was the most dangerous century the world has known because it married the greatest political ambition with the greatest technological achievement. Though the close of the twentieth century saw the threat of totalitarianism blunted, we must understand the part that enthusiasm for social leveling played in its rise. Furthermore, we must continue to oppose it as it returns with ever softer and friendlier faces.

---

1. Jacques Maritain, *Man and the State* (Washington, DC: Catholic University of America Press, 1998), 187.

Seven

THE FAITH OF THE FIXER

A few years back I was very glad to have the opportunity to speak at an event honoring Charles W. Colson, better known as Chuck. In a recent conversation, a friend of mine suggested that Colson was one of the greatest men of the last hundred years. I found myself thinking that he might be right.

When I was in law school in the late 1990s, I decided I wanted to spend a summer working for Prison Fellowship. The organization invited me to a winter conference as a way to meet me and maybe conduct an informal interview. What I remember most about the conference was the first evening. I stood in a room full of people mingling when suddenly I caught the figure of Chuck Colson striding across the room. In previous years, I had been through a pretty intense period of fascination with him and his books.[1] I watched him walking and felt as though an angel had just crossed the room. I guess other people feel that way about athletes or movie stars. Although I did not meet Mr. Colson at the conference, I did get my summer job. Later

---

1. The best known of his books is *Born Again*, but others such as *Loving God* and *How Now Shall We Live?* have also been influential.

that year I would have the opportunity to write a few commercials he recorded for a religious liberty campaign that Prison Fellowship was conducting, and I had a couple of brief conversations with him. Prison Fellowship was lobbying for a bill called the Religious Liberty Protection Act. When we visited members of Congress, we had a reliable tactic to get the best reception possible. For the staffs of Democratic members, we announced ourselves as representatives of Prison Fellowship. When we showed up at Republican quarters, we said we were from Chuck Colson's office. Both names, Prison Fellowship and Chuck Colson, opened doors.

This amazing man built a respected and enduring prison ministry while he simultaneously became a tutor of Christian hearts and minds through his writing, speaking, and broadcasting. The social movement sometimes referred to as the religious Right benefitted tremendously from his good example and from his way of thinking. He is already missed. The ranks of politically involved and devout Christians have suffered the loss of stalwarts such as Colson, Neuhaus, and Buckley in these past few years.

The Chuck Colson I want to talk about now is the younger man, the Colson of the Nixon White House—the Hatchet Man. The aide so loyal that he supposedly once said he would run over his own grandmother to help Richard Nixon. I want to talk about how Chuck Colson became an exemplar of the secular age in which he rose to prominence and how he broke free of the soul-damaging logic of the system he once embraced.

When we talk about the early Chuck Colson—the one with whom American political reporters were once obsessed, and the purported dark figure pulling strings in a White House not known for purity and light—we have to talk about politics as an activity. Is it a field of endeavor with its own logic and rules, independent from some higher law or morality? Is it in reality a deadly serious game concerned with getting and keeping power? There is a lot of pretty talk about the rights of citizens, patriotism, justice, equality, the blessings of God, the city on a hill, and other political bromides, but, in the end, is politics primarily an activity in which one acts in a supremely pragmatic way by rewarding friends and punishing enemies in a kind of cynical calculus of rule?

These questions regularly confront us. And before we are too quick to dismiss them as overwrought or excessively negative, we might remember the drama surrounding Illinois Governor Rod Blagojevich, who tried to sell a senate seat appointment that was his to make. Economic gain is not always the driving force. It may come down to doing what is necessary to make sure that the right people come out on top rather than wrong-thinking enemies. What is permissible under those circumstances? Chuck Colson faced that kind of question many times.

Sociologists of religion have long written and spoken about the theory of secularization. The theory has three branches. The first is pure religious decline. This is the thought that as we become more modern, the number of religious adherents will go down. The jury is still out on that part of the theory, but it is far less confidently proclaimed now than it once was.

The second part of the theory is privatization of religion. In other words, individuals continue to be religious, but they engage in those activities privately. They do not bring them into the public square or into a modern business, for example. This second part of the theory is often seen as an accompaniment or predecessor to the first. In other words, people take their beliefs into their private lives exclusively, and then they or their children eventually stop believing. This part of the theory has definitely suffered reverses. Examples given in José Casanova's distinguished study *Public Religions in the Modern World* include the rise of the Catholic Solidarity worker's union in Poland, the Iranian revolution, and the sudden emergence of conservative Protestants in American politics. All three of those examples occurred in the late 1970s. It also happens that Chuck Colson's *Born Again* (a book that helped challenge secularization indirectly) was published in 1976.

The third branch of the theory, and the part that we are interested in here for the way it is reflected in Colson's story, is functional differentiation. It happens to be the part of the theory that is most widely accepted, even by those sociologists who are skeptical of secularization generally.

What is functional differentiation? It is the idea that modern societies have many different spheres of activity, each of which operates according to its own essentially internal logic. These spheres could be things like business, politics, warfare, science, medicine, sport, and academia. Each has a primary goal toward which it strives. Business is primarily concerned with maximizing profits. Politics is largely directed toward winning and exercising power. Science aims to expand the borders of our knowledge through exploration and experimentation. We could come up with several more examples.

Now, the claims to independence for these various spheres are not absolute, but they are strong. For example, those who offer ethical objections to a particular practice made possible by scientific progress are often pilloried as being antiscience. They are wrongly criticized, though. One would not have to be anticar to object to driving on the sidewalk. In any case, functional differentiation means that a broader set of values, such as natural law or Christianity, does not have the right to meddle in the affairs of these different areas. Indeed, it means that in a more advanced society, such meddling *should not and will not occur.*

There are some advantages to functional differentiation. For example, it may provide more freedom for innovation, dynamism, and new efficiencies. Some have speculated that it actually benefits the church by removing it from many areas of activity that are outside its normal zone of expertise.

There may be times, though, when it is not such a good thing to allow the logic of functional differentiation to prevail. Those who object to religious interference with science may simultaneously applaud religious interference when it comes to the practice of warfare. Functionally differentiated warfare would be a terrible thing to behold. The classical and Christian idea of just war is a limitation on such a practice. Functionally differentiated science can be terrible, too. Freed by the conviction that Jews were subhuman, Nazi scientists allowed their scientific interests to have free rein. Experiments that would previously have been considered outrageous and immoral were carried out at great cost to their subjects.

Observing this dynamic, Casanova has noted that religion serves as "a protector of human rights and humanist values against the secular spheres and their absolute claims to internal functional autonomy."[2]

_____

2. José Casanova, *Public Religions in the Modern World* (Chicago: University of Chicago Press, 1994), 39.

This is the same scholar who has attributed the severe decline of European churches to their attempt to "prolong Christendom ... and resist functional differentiation."[3] Where does this leave us? The church must not attempt to provide religious hall monitor-like supervision to the varied activities of life, but, at the same time, it must oppose functional differentiation that goes too far. In fact, Casanova says that the churches that raise a protest against excessive differentiation actually become stronger in the process. If the church exercises too much control, then the world views it with cynicism. If it exercises too little, it is irrelevant.[4] These two poles are perhaps illustrated historically by, on the one hand, the Catholic Church in Machiavelli's age (which tried to control too much while it was being simultaneously corrupted by and resented by the world) and, on the other hand, the mainline churches in our own day, which mostly seem to simply reflect the dominant sensibilities of the age.

In the case of Chuck Colson, we can see the conflict between the church and functional differentiation played out in the life of one man. Colson's chosen vocation was, broadly, the law, but, more specifically, politics. Although he had a successful law firm, he made his mark as a political operative, first for United States Senator Leverett Saltonstall in Massachusetts, and then for Richard Nixon as special counsel to the president.

What is the nature of differentiated politics? The English sociologist David Martin suggests that "politics is about many things, such as the negotiation of rival interests, but minimally it is about power and potential violence." Martin goes on to outline some of the different roles available to those who participate in politics as a vocation. One of the roles is "fixer."[5] It is probably not unfair to label Colson as a very high-level kind of fixer. He was the person who would do things that were needed to maximize the fortunes of those on his team.

Chuck Colson knew this about himself. In *Born Again*, he reflected on how proud his father had been when President Nixon personally praised Colson's work in the White House. Colson wrote, "I knew, as

3. Casanova, *Public Religions*, 29.

4. Casanova, *Public Religions*, 39.

5. David Martin, *On Secularization: Toward a Revised General Theory* (Aldershot, UK: Ashgate, 2005), 105.

Dad did not, that if I was as valuable to the President as he said I was, it was because I was willing at times to blink at certain ethical standards, to be ruthless in getting things done."[6] The media seemed to perceive this element in Colson's role. A *Wall Street Journal* headline in October 1971 read: NIXON HATCHET MAN CALL IT WHAT YOU WILL, CHUCK COLSON HANDLES PRESIDENT'S DIRTY WORK.

The role of the fixer is not something Colson developed upon arriving as an idealist in the Nixon White House. Rather, it was a role to which he was already well accustomed. He described how he improvised a brilliant campaign trick to save the Massachusetts Republican Senator Saltonstall in 1960, a year in which Irish votes for Kennedy would surely be in abundance. Colson's plan was to find every Irish sounding name in the Boston phone book and mail each of them a letter in which six Democrats endorsed a combination of Kennedy and Saltonstall. He put a bunch of college kids in hotel rooms stuffing envelopes at a frenzied pace the week before the election. They would mail the letters just in time for families to receive them on the Monday before the election. Saltonstall's Democratic opponent (the natural beneficiary of a big Kennedy turnout) would have no time to respond. While not illegal, the tactic was shady, and Colson took pains to make sure Saltonstall knew nothing of it. In fact, he was willing to go a bit too far in order to save his scheme when it looked as though the conscience of one of the female students would get in the way of its execution. Colson recounted how a staff member notified him of the problem:

> "I'm worried about one of our girls. Her father is an avid party man and she thinks we're being disloyal to Nixon. I overheard her talking about going to Republican headquarters to tell the chairman what's going on here."
>
> "Oh, no," I moaned. "That'll blow us right out of the water. Any publicity and this will boomerang. Nixon hasn't a chance in this state and I've told his people what we're doing. We're trying to save a Republican senator, that's all."
>
> I stood with my head down staring at the grease-stained carpet, a sick feeling in my stomach. We couldn't let anyone know that Saltonstall's committee was behind the mailing. It

6. Charles Colson, *Born Again* (Old Tappen, NJ: Chosen Books, 1985), 57.

had to look independent, a genuine letter from Kennedy supporters. The election could be riding on this one last-minute appeal which our opponent would never have time to rebut.

"Tell you what, Tom," I looked up into his tired eyes. "Take this." I handed him ten crisp ten-dollar bills, all I had in my wallet. "Take this girl out tonight and get her loaded. Keep her diverted, whatever you have to do until Election Day."[7]

For those who were not adults during Watergate or who have not read *Born Again* in quite a while (or who have not read it at all), the Colson depicted here is far removed from the one who would play quite a different role in the American consciousness as the years rolled on.

Colson related another story that helps us to understand his life in the White House. This one has to do with Arthur Burns, chairman of the Federal Reserve, whom Nixon appointed to the post in 1970. Still in his first term, Nixon was dissatisfied with Burns' unwillingness to put a rosy face on the state of the economy. When one official pointed out that Burns had been trying to have the Fed chairmanship treated as a cabinet position, Nixon told Colson to leak the story so as to undercut Burns. They would sell it as though Burns were seeking a raise for himself. It would then appear as if Burns, who had been preaching wage and price controls, was trying to feather his own nest. Colson dutifully complied despite some personal misgivings. When it turned out that Burns had not been trying to improve his own position, but that of his successor, the decision to leak the story took on the additional moral freight of being an unsubstantiated lie. Later, when the Watergate controversy was dominating national coverage, the Burns story entered the national news in a column by Tom Braden, whom some may remember as the original inspiration for the Dick Van Patten show *Eight is Enough*, and also as the first occupant of the chair on the left for the CNN debate show *Crossfire*. Braden noted that Colson had apologized to Burns, and he tartly concluded the column by suggesting that Colson had many other people in town to whom he should apologize.

Politics has been referred to as a species of warfare. It is considered to be a tough undertaking. Chris Matthews branded his book and

---

7. Colson, *Born Again*, 28–29.

television show *Hardball*, suggesting the no-holds-barred, people-may-get-hurt nature of politics. It is a competitive endeavor. Politics has very clear winners and losers. It also has zero-sum aspects that make winning and losing highly consequential for the participants. Being in the majority typically means having power. Being in the minority means marginalization. There are friends and enemies. A person can be judged on the basis of the label next to their name.

Perhaps it should not be surprising, then, that the Nixon White House developed the internal logic of politics in such a way that they competed very vigorously and were willing to stretch, and sometimes exceed, the limits in order to win. Colson recalled one evening in Nixon's first term when Nixon's inner circle cruised the Potomac in the presidential yacht, *Sequoia*. At first, Colson's description is touching. The group sat down to a sumptuous meal of steaks and fresh corn on the cob. Nixon tucked a napkin into his collar to protect his tie. The small detail did not escape the class-conscious Colson, who took some pride in Nixon's humble upbringing and who himself had come from a struggling family. They went on to have a policy discussion in which Nixon and Henry Kissinger displayed their brilliance. But before the evening ended, the tone shifted in a more negative direction as they concerned themselves with the political opposition. Colson wrote, "And so on the *Sequoia* this balmy spring night, a Holy War was declared against the enemy—those who opposed the noble goals we sought of peace and stability in the world. *They* who differed with *us*, whatever their motives, must be vanquished. The seeds of destruction were by now already sown—not in them but in us."[8] It is interesting that Colson employed the term "Holy War." As David Martin has noted, in differentiated politics there may well be crusades, but the cross will not be in evidence.[9]

Reflecting on their attitude and their practice, Colson concluded that they had developed a refinement on the old political spoils system, which had been designed to reward friends. The new twist came in the form of an enemies list. It was at this point, Colson said, that they began to "plunge across the moral divide."[10]

---

8. Colson, *Born Again*, 45.

9. Martin, *On Secularization*, 186.

10. Colson, *Born Again*, 61.

In terms of the key metric in politics—winning office—Colson and the Nixon team achieved what every White House team wants. They won a second term with the kind of mandate that came from a massive, landslide victory over George McGovern, who had been successfully tagged as the candidate of amnesty, abortion, and acid. Nixon had the support of the Teamsters union and construction workers. It seemed as though the president and his advisers had turned a corner and were reconfiguring American politics into a new populist, Republican majority.

Yet, in the midst of this triumph, there was very little joy. The following passages are from Colson's arresting account of the election night victory celebration.

> For three long years I had committed everything I had, every ounce of energy to Richard Nixon's cause. Nothing else had mattered. We had had no time together as a family, no social life, no vacations. So why could my tongue not taste the flavor of this hour of conquest?[11]
>
> If someone had peered in on us that night from some imaginary peephole in the ceiling of the President's office, what a curious sight it would have been: a victorious President, grumbling over words he would grudgingly say to his fallen foe; his chief of staff angry, surly, and snarling; and the architect of his political strategy sitting in a numbed stupor.[12]

Why so dark? Why would such a great victory yield so little happiness and satisfaction? I think the answer lies in the nature of differentiated politics as embraced by Nixon and advisers like Colson. It affected their souls. Politics, as they practiced it, had damaged them. They had indeed conducted a crusade with no evidence of the cross in sight. Some victories may not be worth having.

The second term, of course, ended prematurely, with Nixon in disgrace. It tested the one value Colson named as the key to being a political operative at the highest level. "Loyalty," he wrote, "is what being a White House aide is all about. Presidents couldn't survive without loyal aides and I'd been one blindly for so long. There the

---

11. Colson, *Born Again*, 14.

12. Colson, *Born Again*, 17.

gospel began. There it ended."[13] This high value of loyalty is not unique to Republicans. In response to the Monica Lewinsky crisis of the Clinton administration, the prominent Democrat James Carville wrote a book titled *Stickin': The Case for Loyalty*. In it, he favorably cited the example of the nineteenth-century British prime minister Lord Melbourne. A colleague promised Melbourne he would support him as long as he was in the right. Melbourne was dissatisfied: "What I want is men who will support me when I am in the wrong."[14]

In the midst of the Watergate crisis, it rankled Colson that White House Counsel John Dean, who testified against Nixon, had broken the loyalty commandment, while he himself had kept it. Politics has its own code. Colson was still one of the faithful.

Something happened that changed everything for Chuck Colson. It became the title of what remains his most famous book. He was *born again*. There is something amazing about the fact that in a book with scenes from the White House, a diplomatic trip to the Soviet Union, the presidential yacht, and tense legal proceedings, perhaps the most memorable moment occurs with Colson, alone, sitting in his car in the driveway of Tom Phillips, the CEO of Raytheon. Moments before, Phillips had shared the gospel with Colson and had read to him from C. S. Lewis' work on pride. Colson was pierced, but he had hesitated, and was unable to pray with Phillips to receive Christ. And now he sits in his car, leans on the steering wheel, and weeps. He wonders to himself, "What kind of weakness is this?" He wants to go back into the house, but cannot because Phillips and his wife have turned off the lights and retired for the night. Colson steers out of the driveway, crying so hard he is unable to see. He pulls off onto the shoulder and hopes that the Phillipses cannot hear him. Martin Luther had his simple prayer: "I am yours. Save me." Colson's prayer was simpler still: "Take me."[15] It was a surrender of personal pride and personal prerogatives to the lordship of Christ. And with that surrender, he ended his loneliness—perhaps the kind of loneliness that seemed to haunt Nixon in Colson's narrative.

---

13. Colson, *Born Again*, 104.

14. James Carville, *Stickin': The Case for Loyalty* (New York: Simon & Schuster, 2000), 16–17.

15. Colson, *Born Again*, 116–17.

Colson's submission to the lordship of Christ brought an end to a career in which the logic of differentiation held sway. He did what he could to make up for acts that made sense in terms of political warfare, but which were immoral. He apologized to Arthur Burns. He repented of his role in attempting to smear Daniel Ellsberg, and was convicted of obstruction of justice for that attempt, on his own suggestion. A man whom he had once considered an enemy, Democratic Senator Harold Hughes, became his brother in Christ and a staunch ally.

In an interview with Mike Wallace on *60 Minutes*, Colson, with Hughes at his side, realized he could not live in both worlds any more. He could not be both a political aide playing defense and a fully submitted Christian. Under Wallace's tough questioning, Colson appeared evasive. Wallace remarked, "It seems as though your prior faith takes precedence over your new faith."[16] That, of course, encapsulates the entire point of this chapter. Colson had to exchange a highly pragmatic and worldly faith—one that had taken him a long way—for a new faith—one with extensive claims upon his whole life. After the interview, Colson recalled Dietrich Bonhoeffer, who wrote that "to stay in the old situation makes discipleship impossible."[17]

Upon his conviction for obstruction of justice, Colson faced a swarm of reporters and their microphones. His words appear now to have been prophetic: "What happened in court today was the court's will and the Lord's will—I have committed my life to Jesus Christ and I can work for him in prison as well as out."[18] In prison in Alabama, he found himself tempted to follow his old playbook and to work according to the differentiated nature of the institution. Upon reflection, however, he did the things he felt God was calling him to do. He eschewed any kind of deception. More important, he decided to disregard advice to keep his head down and not help the men with their legal problems. He saw the decision as a time to go Christ's way rather than the world's way. Differentiation and compartmentalization gave way to Christ's lordship and the integrated life.

---

16. Colson, *Born Again*, 219.

17. Colson, *Born Again*, 223.

18. Jonathan Aitken, *Charles W. Colson: A Life Redeemed* (New York: Random House, 2010), 247–48.

He noticed that the prisons seemed to have lost their godly purpose. The word *penitentiary* refers to a spiritual state of mind. It should be a place to reflect upon wrongs done and to seek to correct them. Colson noticed that his prison in Alabama appeared to care only about using the prisoners to provide cheap labor. God had put him in prison, he believed, so that he could understand what it meant to lose one's freedom. He would go from being an advocate for the most powerful man in the world to pressing the cause of the most despised and marginalized men in America. Rather than treating them like some interest group, he wanted to address their souls. We know this is how Prison Fellowship was born.

I do not know whether Colson followed the debates over secularization theory or was conversant in the matter of functional differentiation. It would not have been strange if he had, given his associations with various Christian intellectuals. Consciously or not, he went on to conduct a battle against differentiation for the rest of his life. Prison Fellowship was sometimes accused of trying to overstep the bounds between church and state, but that was a misunderstanding. Colson was instead working against the separation of Christianity from life in the world.

During the last four decades, there have been at least three major evangelical movements aimed at the reform of the culture. One effort has been to organize Christians politically. Colson was part of that effort, but it was never his main focus. Another project has been to raise the intellectual bar among evangelicals. Colson encouraged that kind of formation. I am fairly certain that he would have approved of the explosion of Christian classical schools, for example, and renewed attention to the great books. But the third movement is the one that I think really energized Colson and most clearly captures much of his time and effort after Watergate. That third movement has been the battle against functional differentiation. To state it positively, we could say that Chuck Colson fought to convince Christians of their need to live an integrated life. A Christian must never lead the kind of existence like that of a very famous CEO in Houston, who ran a massive corporation that perpetrated a gigantic fraud while he simultaneously was a member in good standing at Second Baptist Church.

It has been said that Chuck was always a marine. In *How Now Shall We Live?*, Colson perfectly summed up both the present chapter and the great lesson of his life's experience and work as he described a question he received after lecturing to a group of marines:

> The last question was the toughest by far. "Mr. Colson," said a master sergeant, "which is more important—loyalty or integrity?"
>
> Now, a marine lives by the creed *semper fidelis*—"always faithful"—and when I was a marine, I learned that loyalty meant unquestioning obedience. Yet I wish I had pondered the young sergeant's question when I was in the Nixon White House. For now I know the answer.
>
> "Integrity comes first," I said. Loyalty, no matter how admirable, can be dangerous if it is invested in an unworthy cause.
>
> *Integrity* comes from the verb *to integrate*, which means to become united so as to form a complete or perfect whole.... Our actions must be consistent with our thoughts. We must be the same person in private and in public.[19]

Chuck Colson was determined to share with everyone what God taught him after he left the Nixon White House. Even now, there are some who think Colson was nothing more than an opportunist in his public conversion to Christ. But I submit to you that he was a very intelligent man who learned the lesson that God taught him. He learned it so well that he went from being merely a very clever man to being a wise and loving servant of God's kingdom.

---

19. Charles Colson and Nancy Pearcey, *How Now Shall We Live?* (Wheaton, IL: Tyndale House, 1999), 379.

Eight

SHOULD CHRISTIANS
BE SILENT FOR A SEASON?

In the pages of the *Journal of Markets & Morality*,[1] Jonathan Malesic and I debated the merits of secularism as the proper mode of cultural engagement for Christians. He pointed to Christians who might be considered elites in terms of worldly success and noted that they actually appear to wrongly use their faith as a networking and marketing tool. Malesic, dissatisfied with what he observed, offered a prescription. Rather than trumpet their faith and seek the public support of fellow believers, he argued, believers should embrace a form of secularism and begin a new life as secret Christians. By secret Christians, Malesic meant to suggest a spiritual discipline of sorts. Christians should live their faith without being so noisy about it.

There is some intuitive appeal to that point of view; nevertheless, Malesic's prescription surprised me because it ran counter to one of the great priorities of the last thirty years of Christian ministry, activism, and advocacy, which has been to resist the privatization of the faith. Rather than accepting the old nostrum that religion is

---

1. "Is Some Form of Secularism the Best Foundation for Christian Engagement in Public Life?" *Journal of Markets & Morality* 13, no. 2 (2010): 347–70.

one of the two things (politics is the other) that do not make for good dinner conversation and are not topics for cocktail parties, a variety of Christian voices have prevailed to some degree in their effort to call on their fellow religionists to stand up and be counted. This movement toward public Christianity has been a conscious response to the academic, media, and cultural avant-garde that proclaims the progressive extinction of religion in our lives and seeks to isolate faith as some kind of vestigial force in public life. Religion, in their view, is like the appendix. They cannot discern a useful purpose for it, and they hope the evolution of the species will eventually delete it so they will not have to countenance its disconcerting presence any longer.

Another driver of the counterrevolution by Christians and churches determined to push their flocks out into the offices, streets, factories, stores, and the like, as identifiable Christians has been massive social change. *Roe v. Wade* is a prime example. Although evangelicals slept during the early 1970s, Francis Schaeffer, among others, eventually succeeded in pricking the dormant social and political conscience of evangelicals. Deprivatization was part of the response. Had they been more alive to the relationship between faith and public life, many probably wondered, would such disastrous sexual and reproductive seeds have bloomed as they did at such great cost? In any case, the mainstream press was shocked to see the sudden emergence of so many public Christians. The self-identification of elite men such as the disgraced Nixon aide Chuck Colson and President Jimmy Carter as "born-again Christians," combined with a surge in Christian political activity, served stunning notice that deprivatization was afoot. Where had these people come from?

It has now become part of the expectation of serious Christians that they ought to be willing to be known as such. Their public self-identification often functions less as a triumphalistic or egotistic expression of the type that Malesic abhors, than it does as something that draws unwelcome attention to the self-identifier. I recall my own time as a law student at the University of Houston. Although my occasional advocacy and defense of the faith in the classrooms of seventy to eighty students was sometimes uncomfortable, I discovered that in moments when I could be found alone, such as in a corner of the library or walking to my car in the parking lot, fellow Christians would seek me out to thank me for representing their point of view.

They felt the same burden to speak out that I did, but were often afraid of doing so and thus being ridiculed or held in contempt by others. In many worldly contexts, making one's Christian identity known can be like wearing the tonsure haircut of monks. Many Christians have learned hard lessons while bearing this responsibility. When we speak, we should do so standing on firm ground, closely guided by relevance, and taking care to speak with information and sophistication to the degree we are able to achieve it. My own early mistakes and my shame at the missteps of others have spurred me to work hard at developing a social witness that is winsome and truthful. It is not enough to merely proclaim.

It may be the case that one must stand up and be counted in order to encourage one's fellow believers and to make sure that the Christian witness and worldview are at least made known to the broader community. But there is a larger controversy lurking behind the first. Should we go beyond bearing witness to actively trying to change the world through activities such as politics, education, mass media, and the arts?

In the 1970s, Francis Schaeffer brought his knickers and chin beard to America for memorable discussions about *Whatever Happened to the Human Race?* and *How Shall We Then Live?* Since that time, conservative evangelicals and Catholics have been working hard to develop a solid Christian worldview and to advance the kingdom of Christ in the broader culture by redeeming the culture's values. Their effort has been strategic and aimed at procuring victory.

Operating with the recent memory of an era when terms like *divorce, abortion,* and *living together* were widely considered shocking and scandalous, generations of Christians since the latter third of the twentieth century have labored toward restoration with the sense that a better past was not too far in the rearview mirror to be recovered. Although that recovery may have seemed tantalizingly close, those of us in the movement may have failed to notice that while the years in which a more Christian lifestyle had been normative were not so far away, it had indeed been a long time since the most important intellectuals and cultural institutions were meaningfully faithful.

Now, clearly no longer a dominant cultural force, Christians have to decide how to move forward. Should they find a way to aggregate all the culturally conservative groups (Orthodox Jews, serious

Catholics, evangelicals, Muslims, and others) so as to put together a simple majority of 50 percent plus one?

In his frequently cited book *To Change the World*, James Davison Hunter provocatively asserts that the Christian account of changing the world, which includes holding the right values, thinking Christianly, and having courage, "is almost wholly mistaken." Hunter, a sociologist, notes that after reaching a high point of prestige and influence in the nineteenth century the influence of the church has been declining for 175 years. The decline has occurred despite the presence of tens of millions of enthusiastic Christians in American society making efforts to transform the culture. At the same time, minorities such as Jews and gays (both of which work from far smaller numerical bases) have made gigantic strides in developing their own cultural influence and power.[2]

So, why might it be the case that Christians have lost influence while much smaller niche groups such as Jews and gays have radically increased their own power to shape culture? The answer, according to Hunter, is that Christians have misunderstood the levers of change. Christians have assumed that ideas alter history and that a sufficient effort to get certain ideas into circulation will move the world. Hunter argues that cultural formation is largely the result of institutions, structures of power, and networks of influence. While Christians have created some impressive institutions in places like Colorado Springs, Wheaton, and Waco, they do not compare to the power conferred by New York or Los Angeles. In other words, according to Hunter's analysis, Christian institutions, publications, and creations of popular culture emanate from the periphery rather than the center. And the center is where the real power and symbolic capital are found. Although Hunter does not say as much, one suspects that the Left's great desire to marginalize and undercut Fox News as a media organization stems from its existence in New York as a nonconforming major player in a business once operated almost completely by a particular kind of elite sensibility. Fox News gives conservatism a platform in the center of media power that Christians still do not have, and do not have any prospect of possessing.

---

2. James Davison Hunter, *To Change the World* (New York: Oxford University Press, 2010), 17–21.

Thus, Christians have their *Books and Culture* and their *Christianity Today* emanating from Wheaton, Illinois, but neither can compare to the influence of *The New York Times Review of Books* or *The New Yorker*. Interestingly, Hunter singles out *First Things* (created and published in New York) as the one seriously Christian entity to achieve significant influence among elites. (Then again, even *First Things* is an order of magnitude below something like the joint dream of Billy Graham and Carl F. H. Henry to build a world-class Christian university in the Big Apple.) The overall point here is that while Christians have built strength on the periphery, it does not matter nearly as much as being able to apply leverage at the center. And the center is important because that is where real power lives. As much as we want to extol the grass roots and populism, real cultural change (in Hunter's account) works from the top down and is driven by elites (often alternative elites) who are able to penetrate the highest and most concentric of social circles. The formula is to create overlapping networks of elites in spheres of culture working together with great persistence.

Hunter proves his analysis through reference to the history of the church, noting that the great church fathers frequently came from elite families and had training in Greek, Latin, rhetoric, and jurisprudence. These individuals were able to engage center-elites with a high quality and quantity of intellectual output. The apostle Paul, of course, was one of the first of this breed. See his challenge to the men of Athens at the Areopagus in which he used his understanding of the dominant culture in order to challenge it. Rodney Stark's case in *The Rise of Christianity* agrees with Hunter's. Stark argues that Christianity was not primarily a lower class or slave religion (driven forward by its ability to load the powerful with guilt and to assuage the natural inferiority of its adherents, as some Enlightenment thinkers argued), but that, instead, it was embraced by and spread in significant part thanks to the influence of many in the upper echelons of society. Hunter also points out that missionaries often converted those in the top tier of society first, because doing so created protection for people lower in the social order who could then convert with less risk to their lives.

He traces the phenomenon through the Reformation, which we think of as a highly popular movement. In Hunter's telling, alternative elites such as Luther and Calvin used their powerful learning in the areas of classics and Christianity to bring a leading edge of modified Christian culture and intellect into contact with sources of social power. Their movement required the safe haven offered by various nobles. Without it, the reform would likely have been snuffed out. Similarly, an alternative elite consisting of men like the Wesleys, George Whitefield, and Jonathan Edwards brought about the Great Awakening. So, too, did social change come about through William Wilberforce's elites working together in the Clapham Circle to bring about the end of slavery in England.

The same dynamic applies to those who are outside the Christian faith. It is true that the universities were once almost exclusively Christian in both their composition and their outlook. Working from a series of alternative institutions such as salons, literary clubs, and royal academies in the seventeenth and eighteenth centuries, Enlightenment-oriented elites were able to penetrate and transform the universities.

The key to world changing is not to impose a cultural agenda, but to start by creating space for a new way of living and thinking. Challenge the established circles. Penetrate them. Redefine the norms. This is a far better approach to the brute force method of political organizing. The best example to consider in that paradigm is Prohibition. It was arguably public Christianity's greatest politico-legal success in American history, and its greatest failure. Temperance activists were able to move the votes, but failed to change the underlying cultural assumptions. Thus, the reform did not last.

Even if a group does succeed in winning the cultural battle, Hunter warns that it cannot really control the outcome. The partisans of Enlightenment, in their great desire to see scientific advance, would never have desired the creation and use of nuclear weapons, for example. Yet, the focus on scientific development has led to both the subjugation and endangerment of the physical order.

With the book's first essay, Hunter achieves three purposes. He describes what is actually required to change the world, explains how Christians are failing to do what is required, and warns against the focus on gaining power to effect change. It is also in the first essay that he briefly mentions the model of cultural engagement he endorses, namely, faithful presence.[3]

Whether or not one agrees with Hunter's conclusions, the discussion of how cultural change can actually be achieved is invaluable and should serve as the source of much self-examination and strategic reconsideration among those in the "taking back the culture for Christ" industry. If the reader finds Hunter convincing on this score (as I do), then it is time to de-emphasize the political program, fire the consultants who teach you how to write a good appeal letter that features breathless and apocalyptic zeal, and figure out how to create room to breathe and work inside the key center zones of culture. Christian philanthropists should pay special attention as they consider efforts for possible investment. The effort to establish The King's College as a niche college operation in Manhattan is not a bad example of the strategy at work.

The question on the table, though, is whether Christians should, in fact, make a conscious effort to change the world via a strategy of working within the centers of power. Hunter did not write his book with the goal of helping Christians to become more sophisticated and to have a higher chance of success in reclaiming the culture. In fact, he explicitly disclaims any such project. His second essay helps explain his reasoning.

We now live in a low-consensus society (Francis Schaeffer pointed to the loss of the "Christian consensus"). As a result, the glue that holds us together comes down to coercive power reposed in the state. Indeed, Hunter provides something like an axiom that could be recited in political science courses: Law increases as cultural consensus decreases. Though we try to pretend that we are avoiding contests about the nature of the good through any number of tortured, academic attempts at neutrality, we are tilting at windmills. Law implies moral judgment. As a result, every faction seeks state power in order to impose its understanding of the good on the whole society. Accordingly, our news reporting focuses largely on our perception of who is winning or losing any given battle. Our public life has become politicized. And the problem is that the state becomes the final arbiter because of its exercise of dominance and control.

---

3. Hunter, *To Change the World*, 95.

Hunter believes that Christians have largely bought into the idea of using politics to bring about our own vision of the good society. The Christian Right is mostly interested in gaining power to retard or even roll back the secularization of society that is evident in the strict separation mode of church-state jurisprudence and changes in sexual morality. Those on the Christian Left hope to employ the machinery of government to bring about greater material equality among citizens. Neo-Anabaptists reject power altogether and model powerlessness in an attempt to create an alternative *civitas* in the form of the church. Despite the neo-Anabaptist rejection of political power, they see their own identity in relation to it.

One of the problems with this elevation of politics is that it depicts public life only in terms of the political. This can lead to irresponsibility. For example, this approach can end up championing child welfare programs instead of doing something much more immediate than state action, such as adopting a child. Making the solution to every problem political is also problematic because of what power does. It tends to become an end rather than a means. It also tends to grow and become inescapable, thus limiting freedom of action and creating a lasting sense of injury in those who feel they have been excluded from power or intruded upon by it.

Hunter's thoughts on power are welcome and needed, and not only among Christians. Much political discourse in the past couple of decades has centered on the special damage done to the political process by religious participants and their rhetoric. Hunter properly recognizes that it is not so much religious power that creates the grievance, but, more properly, simply power that is exercised by someone other than oneself.

Hunter advises that the Christian response to all this should be to "see politics for what it is" and to "decouple the public from the political."[4] As I write those words, I cannot help but think of the distinction I have mentioned already that Thomas Paine drew between society and government. Society is a mode of voluntary cooperation that we undertake because we recognize that we can achieve more by working together. Government, by contrast, is a necessary evil required by the abuses of human freedom. It should be obvious that

---

4. Hunter, *To Change the World*, 185.

the mode of society is far superior and, whenever possible, should be preferred to government. Hunter appears to be arguing in the same vein. The current political platform of the Conservative Party in the UK includes many references to a concept called "the big society," which appears to be based on similar ideas.

Hunter's notion of being able to see the public as something more than the political is important. Weaning the culture from resolving every disputable question with the power of politics is necessary if we are to avoid escalating levels of conflict and resentment. In this connection, however, I think he gives Christian conservatives too little credit. It seems to me that one of the primary goals of the movement has been to keep the responsibility for much of the cooperative aspect of living together within the voluntary mode of society rather than the coercive mode of government. It needs to be remembered that Christian conservatives have been less a force for enacting all kinds of new restrictions in the last half century than they have fought a defensive battle against the advance of a cultural vanguard. Viewed from one perspective, for example, Christian conservatives appear to be foisting their view of marriage on the populace. Considered more realistically, though, one might realize that they are simply protecting one of the most widely assumed social facts and whole-some social institutions in the known history of the world. Outside of this sort of action on behalf of basic ideas such as the meaning of marriage or the sanctity of life, many who fit within the Christian Right believe passionately in voluntary social cooperation and in notions of decentralization and subsidiarity.

In giving up their dependence on politics as a mode of social change, Christians should, according to Hunter, ramp up the sense of their distinctiveness from the dominant culture. The faithful will make their greatest contribution by modeling a way that is different from the functionally differentiated culture that we have all come to accept more fully than we may realize. This means that the churched will live in a noticeably different way and make decisions on a different basis from the broader culture with regard to "courtships, marriage, child-rearing, duty, obligations, consumption, leisure, retirement" and other areas.[5]

---

5. Hunter, *To Change the World*, 184–85.

Hunter's third essay brings together threads of his analysis and attempts to offer a new way forward. Christians have had to adapt to pervasive pluralism. We no longer live under a Bergerian sacred canopy in which it is easy to be a believer because all the social institutions and people around us support our belief. Instead, we are constantly confronted by "multiple and fragmented perspectives."[6] Christianity is no longer the defender of the social order as it was in Europe and then in America for so many centuries. Now Christianity has returned to having the status of a threat, which is how it was viewed in the beginning.

One might expect radical skepticism to be the cultural reaction to an extremely pluralistic environment, but that reaction does not occur because such skepticism is not really livable. Instead, the culture embraces a type of unstated nihilism, which manifests itself as indulgence, acquisition, and spectacle. It is easy to see that Hunter may be right as we observe increasing consumerism, the idolization of celebrity *qua* celebrity, and a growing obsession with any scandal that can be manufactured.

During these challenging times, Christians have too often focused on reconstructing a parallel sacred canopy to replace the one torn apart by modernity. These institutions and ideas can end up working as a segregated sideshow that bolsters the faithful in their beliefs, but fails utterly to directly challenge the centers of culture. Even though one might concede Hunter's point that these institutions and ideas fail to challenge the centers of culture, to some degree, however, these parallel structures do help keep important ideas alive and are often the sorts of places that produce elites who may reach the center. One might think of Wheaton College in the 1960s. Without conducting any research, one might simply recall that Mark Noll (one of the finest historians of religion in America), Nathan Hatch (former provost of Notre Dame and current president of Wake Forest University), David Jeffrey (an impressive literary scholar and hugely important influence on Baylor's institutional ascent), and the well-known philosopher C. Stephen Evans all came out of that small school. And who knows how many others may not come readily to mind, but went on to important positions elsewhere, such as

---

6. Hunter, *To Change the World*, 203.

my father-in-law (a Wheaton scholarship kid from those days) who went on to become dean of libraries at a large state university? One of the important questions that we who are in Christian universities might ask ourselves is whether today's Wheaton has the same formative power as it did in the 1960s. Does Calvin College still have the formative power that it once had? I do not ask these questions to be arch or to insinuate anything negative, but only to offer up the past influence of these institutions as a sort of ideal to which all of us in the Christian universities might aspire.

Hunter's broader point here, though, is that the answer to perceived decline is not to attempt to mobilize numbers and prevail politically through massive organizations so as to gain power in order to impose a better culture upon our fellow citizens. But here we arrive at the point where the scholar's project faces its greatest challenge. Having brought us to a more sophisticated understanding of the cultural situation, the inevitable question is, what should Christians do?

Hunter's answer focuses on the concept of faithful presence. Faithful presence means that Christians should be working toward a vision of shalom, which involves order, harmony, abundance, beauty, joy, and well-being for all people. They should offer critical resistance to those things that do not lead to human flourishing, and they should make an extended effort to retrieve social goods that have been lost or are in danger of being lost. But all of this should be done without any real effort to impose. God does not force us against our will to live in conformity with his law. Faithful presence means that we pursue, identify with, and labor toward the good of others. Our exercise of power must conform to Christ's exercise of power.

What Hunter means by faithful presence, despite the explanation above, is not totally clear. That is not unusual. Sublimities do not often yield to detailed mapping. But my own reading leads me to conclude that faithful presence is something like an extended effort to persuade others and attempt to draw them near by loving them, serving them, and portraying a vision of the good that does not contain the threat of imposition. Certainly, it is clear that Hunter would have Christians completely eradicate anything in their politics that could be viewed as tribal in character. In other words, it must never be "us" *against* the unwashed "them." Instead, it is "us" *for* "them."

And "they" can really feel the benevolence of our intent even if they do not always agree.

Faithful presence is both aspirational and corrective. It is aspirational in the sense that it invites us to create fresh and possibly more productive modes of social engagement. It is corrective insofar as it pulls us away from viewing politics as something akin to college athletics in which one's team is winning or losing and the other side must be defeated.

But questions remain. For example, how can we square this social wooing with the need to speak prophetically and, yes, politically, against clear injustice? He suggests, for example, that Christians should be silent for a season in politics. (It looks as if Hunter's argument has come back around to Jonathan Malesic's position, where we started.) But is that a reasonable thing to say to the pro-life movement? Would it have been an acceptable thing to say to Christian abolitionists or antisegregationists? In addition, he asserts with some confidence that God's kingdom is not political in character. Surely, Jesus did not transform his ministry into a political one during his temporal life on earth, but can we be so sure this kingdom is not political? After all, we are talking about the King of kings, the risen Lord, who is able to take away the most potent weapon of the state, which is death.[7]

In my friendly debate with Malesic over secularism, he objected to some degree to my claim that public Christianity is important because it helps to impart virtue to a given society. He stated that if one builds a case for Christianity in terms of its sociological value, then one sets the faith up for a fall when sociologists are able to compile a study demonstrating no positive impact on the society. While I would not want to premise the value of Christianity on some sociological effectiveness index, I think almost any Christian would be greatly disappointed if such a null impact could be demonstrated. If Christ is Lord of our lives, then our lives should look substantially different. In reality, I think it is not difficult to demonstrate sociologically, historically, anthropologically, economically, and so forth, that the long

---

7. I owe this observation to N. T. Wright who writes forcefully about the resurrection and politics in *The Resurrection of the Son of God* (Minneapolis: Fortess, 2003).

life of Western civilization has been influenced much to the good by the public and vital presence of Christianity, both *de jure* and then *de facto* as part of the culture. If we were to go more strongly in the direction of a secular society, government elites would be stunned at the giant gaps in the areas of health care, higher education, primary education, and various charitable services that would have to be filled by new state institutions.

Neither Hunter's faithful presence nor Malesic's self-imposed silence strikes me as the appropriate response to the cultural moment. Despite his disavowal of the project, James Davison Hunter provides us with the road map on how to change the culture rather than merely existing within it. We should make a more intentional effort to move from periphery to center and to penetrate the ranks of the intellectual class. If the culture moved to where it is via the strategies Hunter describes, then it seems that it could be moved to a different place. Perhaps we could help bring about a culture (to give a few examples) that protects unborn children by cherishing life, cares more deeply about born children by prizing parental commitment, and increases the brotherhood and sisterhood of men and women by pointing to the fatherhood of God. If we must be wiser, then let us be so, but let us also remain ambitious while the sun still shines. As a character in Lewis' *The Great Divorce* notes, "It will be dark presently."[8]

---

8. C. S. Lewis, *The Great Divorce* (New York: HarperCollins, 2009), 15.

Nine

LIBERTARIANS AND SOCIAL CONSERVATIVES: CAN THEY FIND COMMON GROUND?

A s the standard-bearer for American conservatism for two decades, Ronald Reagan effortlessly embodied fusionism by unit-
ing Mont Pelerin–style libertarians, populist Christians, Burkean
conservatives, and national security voters into a devastatingly
successful electoral bloc. Today it is nearly impossible to imagine
a presidential candidate winning both New York and Texas, but
Reagan, with that group of fellow travelers, did.

Since that time, the coalition has begun to show strain as the forces
pushing outward exceeded those that held it together. The Soviet
Union, once so great a threat that Whittaker Chambers felt certain
he was switching to the losing side when he began to inform on fellow
Communist agents working within the United States, evaporated in
what seemed like a period of days in the early 1990s. Suddenly, the
ultimate threat of despotic big government eased and the Reaganite
companions in arms had the occasion to reassess their relationship.
The review of competing priorities has left former friends moving
apart. Perhaps nowhere is the tension greater and more consequential
than between the socially conservative elements of the group and
devotees of libertarianism.

The two groups have little natural tendency to trust each other when not confronted by a common enemy as they were during the Cold War. Libertarians simply want to minimize the role of government as much as possible. For them, questions of maintaining strong traditional family units and preserving sexual or bioethical mores fall into an unessential realm as far as government is concerned. The government, echoing the thought of John Locke, should primarily occupy itself with providing for physical safety of the person while allowing for the maximum freedom possible for pursuit of self-interest.

Social conservatives similarly view the government as having a primary mission of providing safety, but they also look to the law as a source of moral authority. Man-made law, for them, should seek to be in accord to some degree with divine and natural law. Rifts open wide when social conservatives pursue a public policy agenda designed to prevent divorce, encourage marriage over cohabitation, prevent new understandings of marriage from emerging (e.g., gay marriage or polygamous marriage), prevent avant-garde developments in biological experimentation, and a variety of other issues outside (from the libertarian perspective) the true mandate of government, which cannot seek to define the good, the right, and the beautiful for a community of individuals. To the degree social conservatives seek to achieve some kind of collective excellence along the lines suggested by Aristotle and Thomas Aquinas, libertarians see a mirror image of the threat posed by big-government leftists.

Equally intense suspicions exist on the socially conservative side of the relationship. Libertarians can appear to be obsessed with money and a desire to be left alone, unencumbered by any obligation to their fellows other than not to interfere with their lives. The tension inherent in the relationship erupted during the American presidential primaries when the libertarian-oriented Club for Growth clashed with former Arkansas governor Mike Huckabee, a Christian conservative. Club for Growth seemed to single out Huckabee and take the most uncharitable view possible of his free-market bona fides. Rather than attempt conciliation, Huckabee apparently relished the attack and labeled the small-government group as the "Club for Greed."

The question, borrowed from the longest-running feature in women's magazine history, is, can this marriage be saved? Do libertarians and social conservatives with religious concerns have a relationship worth preserving? As a Christian with strong sympathies toward social conservatism, I can help address part of that question. My answer is that libertarians and social conservatives have a strong interest in seeing each other persist in the American polity. Perhaps a libertarian analyst can address the issue from the other side.

So, why should libertarians see value in what social and religious conservatives hope to achieve? The answer lies in the concept at the core of the American experiment. America is not about unfettered freedom. America is about a particular type of liberty that has been the glory of the Western heritage: ordered liberty. Freedom without a strong moral basis ends up being an empty promise. The American founding generation understood the problem very clearly. The solution that appealed to a great many of them was to encourage religion among the American people. In their view, the Christian religion helped make citizens fit for a republican style of government. Meaningful freedom required the exercise of virtue by the citizens. The connection between religion and virtue was easy to make. After all, even Voltaire hid his skeptical conversations about religion from his servants for fear that they would steal the silver if released from the fear of divine punishment.

Put very simply, the travail of freedom is this: Immoral actors take advantage of moral actors. If everyone has to rationally suspect others of immoral behavior in order to protect themselves, then the value of exchange is severely undercut by the cost of self-protective action. Eventually, in an attempt to ease the expense of self-protection, participants petition the government for regulation. Regulation undercuts the entire libertarian idea. The key, of course, to breaking the cycle of advantage-taking and regulation-building is to change the nature of the actors. The more virtuous the actors, the less opportunistic the behavior, and the more confidence all actors can have at the outset of exchange. What is needed is trust. With trust, the costs of transaction rapidly decline and the need for government regulation and enforcement moves downward as well. Social conservatives press for public policies that tend to increase social capital by improving citizens.

For example, consider the social conservative push toward policies that encourage marriage rather than cohabitation and discourage divorce. Social statistics from the last twenty years establish in a fairly uncontroversial fashion that children from intact, two-parent families will, on average, perform better in school, are less likely to get pregnant out of wedlock, are less likely to do drugs or abuse alcohol, and are substantially less likely to spend time in prison. If there are policies that can actually increase the likelihood that children can be raised in intact families, then it makes sense to pursue those policies (within reason) because those children will become, on average, more virtuous citizens who are less likely to impose costs on others through moral failures. If the logic here is sound, then libertarians have an incentive to consider at least some policy activities of social conservatives as potentially justifiable and beneficial even within a libertarian framework.

The crux of the matter is social capital. Social capital is the name we give to the value generated by the virtuous actions and attitudes of the people. A society with a libertarian style of government is a near impossibility without substantial social capital. No trust, no virtue, no small government. This formula is virtually axiomatic.

Another point of connection between libertarians and social and religious conservatives occurs because of theology. Social conservatives tend to believe human beings are tainted by a sinful nature. If we are all sinful, then how sound a policy is it to place a great deal of power in a government consisting of one person or of many persons? Although the Christian revelation, for example, does not aim its canon specifically at monarchy or any other kind of high-powered government, the practical outworking of a doctrine of original sin is that power should be restricted, checked, and divided. The American constitutional regime set up by the founding generation should surprise no one. It was a likely outcome of a group of thinkers not only influenced by Locke, but also by the Calvinism that had long been prominent in the New World as the faith of the Puritans.

This suspicion of power continues to unite social conservatives and libertarians. While libertarians might protest that social conservatives seek to expand the government's interest in "private" matters of sex, reproduction, and marriage, the reality is that conservatives have primarily fought a rearguard action in which they have attempted to preserve laws under attack by an activist judiciary. Social conservatives have not fought for some new regime of moral authority at the expense of freedom. Rather, they have tried to save the old one because of the educational effect of law.

When it comes to new ideas about expanding government, social conservatives remain largely quite reserved exactly because of their desire not to feed a bureaucratic beast that is likely to develop an agenda independent of its intended purpose. As a group, they would far prefer to see mediating institutions take on the great social reforms of the day, just as they would prefer to see the church return to a much more prominent role in addressing both the needs of the poor and the root causes of poverty. Another issue that offers great promise for the relationship between social and religious conservatives and libertarians is school choice. Prior to the terrorist attacks of September 11, the movement for school choice was gaining steam very rapidly. It was the rare initiative that seemed to fit libertarian purposes easily while simultaneously addressing the question of social justice. After September 11, the war on terror sucked all the air out of the room for creative social policy advances, and school choice moved well down the national agenda.

School choice has not gone away, though. It is a matter that promises to reemerge powerfully when domestic policy again moves to center focus. A great many evangelicals probably came to know of Milton Friedman because of his work in school choice rather than because of his justly famous broader work in economic theory. For libertarians the interest comes from harnessing the power of competition to improve the entire educational system and to take a step toward privatizing a massive public undertaking. Social conservatives perceive those virtues, but are more interested in the protection school choice offers for their right to control the education of their children and to insulate them from what they view as the indoctrination of left-wing ideology.

So, can the marriage be saved? Are libertarians and social conservatives destined to grow further apart, or can they unite around these points of connection involving social capital, suspicion of government power, and the privatization of public education? I submit that the points of connection, notwithstanding messy public blowups like the Huckabee–Club for Growth affair, are much stronger than the forces pulling the two groups apart. This survey demonstrates how much they have in common and how fruitful conversation between the two can be.

Ten

THE STATE OF CHRISTIAN HIGHER EDUCATION

O ne of the great grievances of many Christians has to do with the history of higher education in America. Many have heard the story of how the majority of colleges began with Christian foundations and slowly moved away from the faith. Schools changed their hiring policies, their standards of behavior, their leaders, their church affiliations, their curricula, and even their mottos (such as Harvard's change from VERITAS CHRISTO ET ECCLESIAE to VERITAS). Christian higher education in America became simply American higher education.

The transition happened mostly in the twentieth century and is nearly complete. Fabulously wealthy secular private schools and the finest state universities dominate the top tier of American higher education. At the most exclusive institutions, students enjoy spectacular facilities on gorgeous campuses. Their professors have earned their degrees from the most prestigious programs. They labor under strong research and publication expectations, while instruction is often a secondary concern. Many professors at these schools teach no more than two courses per semester (often with assistance from graduate students). Tenure is difficult to achieve. Although the strongest candidates get the assistant professorships, a number of them will fail to get tenure in an up or out process. The model resembles partnership at the kind of law firms one might find in the top floors of skyscrapers.

Two Giants—Catholic and Protestant

Christian colleges and universities exist almost completely outside of this elite world. There are two notable exceptions. The University of Notre Dame is the premier Catholic school in the United States. It has billions of dollars worth of endowment to subsidize its operations and can command hefty tuition prices. Once known mostly for its Fighting Irish football teams, Notre Dame has become one of America's elite universities. The only problem with all of this as it relates to Christian higher education is that Notre Dame's faith identity is somewhat in doubt. While alumni insist that students continue to be devout in dormitories, David Solomon (a longtime professor and faithful critic) notes that Notre Dame hires primarily for purposes of rank rather than with the school's historic mission in mind. In many ways, Notre Dame appears to be belatedly slipping into the two spheres model that eased many Christian colleges into secularization. The two spheres idea is that a Christian school can have a healthy spiritual life through student activities while going after the academic work in a largely secular fashion. But the idea is false. For better or worse, a university *is* its faculty. If professors no longer *profess* the faith, the university will eventually cease to do so as well. Solomon (perhaps in a sign of the times) has been eased out of his role as director of an institute on ethics and culture at Notre Dame.

The other significant exception is Baylor University. Baylor now has a billion dollars in endowment. That amount, for a private university, is probably just about the minimum required to compete financially with the top-tier schools. Baylor embraced the two spheres approach with enthusiasm for decades, but slipped into secularization less fully than might be expected, perhaps because of the university's strong traditional ties with Texas churches. When Robert Sloan, an interim pastor at many different churches in the Lone Star state, became president in 1995, he and others at Baylor realized that the recent break from the Baptist General Convention of Texas might be the final step toward secularization for the university. Sloan and a number of notable persons at Baylor, such as Donald Schmeltekopf, Michael Beaty, David Lyle Jeffrey, and others, worked toward a vision of reinforcing the university's Christian identity while simultaneously reaching for true research university status.

The vision meant big changes for Baylor in a variety of ways. Sloan and top administrators provided substantial oversight over hiring to make sure that new professors were serious about the Christian faith. At the same time, the profile for hiring tilted toward scholars likely to be prolific in research and publication. Existing faculty, long oriented more around teaching, felt concerned that they were being demoted to second-class status. Attempts to reassure them, such as establishing a separate teaching track as a path for promotion and tenure, only exacerbated the problem. The new vision was stressful for the university financially as well. Baylor hired professors at a rapid rate, engaged in ambitious building projects (including a $100 million science building), and reduced teaching loads from three courses a semester to two for research faculty. Caught in the maelstrom of ideological, spiritual, and financial stressors involved, Sloan resigned after ten years as president. Providentially, it seems, the plan has worked and Baylor today is strong, financially successful, and more intentional about its faith. Although Baylor has not yet reached Notre Dame's level of success, it has become a major university and arguably excels Notre Dame as a Christian institution in the sense that faith remains a major consideration in hiring. Should Baylor put together a few football seasons like the one it has recently strung together (with a Heisman winner to boot), the sky would be the limit. (I am kidding only a very little bit.)

Based on the historical patterns, Notre Dame appears to be a candidate for secularization while Baylor is something different. It is different in the sense that it self-consciously reversed course against secularization and in the nature of its ambition. Mark Noll once told me that Baylor undertook the journey Wheaton College chose against. In other words, Baylor decided to be a comprehensive Protestant university with full-scale research, scholarship, NCAA Division I athletics, and funded graduate education. It is now *sui generis*, unique.

Christian Colleges in the Current Educational Environment

The rest of the Protestant and evangelical Christian colleges and universities with serious spiritual missions are either older schools that somehow avoided the massive wave of secularization that hit the sector in the early to mid-twentieth centuries (probably thanks to heroic leadership in many cases) and relative newcomers (say, less than seventy years old) founded as a direct answer to secularization. How do these institutions fare?

Allen Guelzo, a brilliant and much-decorated Abraham Lincoln scholar who is also a believer, wrote a piece for *Touchstone* in 2011 in which he delivered a largely negative verdict on Christian higher education.[1] Guelzo pointed out a number of troubling issues, such as that few of the schools are selective, alumni are not giving, and many of the schools are in bad financial condition despite the continued rise in tuition rates. His verdict is both right and wrong.

It is true that most Christian colleges lack significant endowments and rely heavily upon tuition in order to fund operations. This fact is disturbing because Christian colleges do not have a business-type mission of making money or acquiring a dominating market share. Really, they just want to offer a distinctively Christian education to students. They would prefer to have the option of discontinuing tuition, which was an idea Harvard flirted with prior to the 2008 crash. The reality, however, is that Christian colleges simply do not have the means to operate tuition free. They are able to offer some scholarships and tuition discounting, but it would be much better to be able to give the students more generous packages. Denominational aid to Christian colleges has been a traditional source of student scholarships, but such assistance has declined in real dollars over time.

On a related front, Guelzo is also correct about a lack of alumni giving at many Christian colleges. But there are good reasons for the perceived lack of later financial attention from many alumni. The dominant one is that graduates from Christian colleges serious

---

1. Allen Guelzo, "Course Corrections: Whither the Evangelical Colleges?" *Touchstone* 24, no. 3 (2011), http://www.touchstonemag.com/archives/article. php?id=24-03-029-f.

about their faith spend the rest of their lives with charitable obligations that they consider to be prior to the needs of the school. I am thinking of the obligation to tithe. Students from families serious enough about their faith to want a Christian education are also committed to their churches. They give to churches, to missions, to Bible translation, and to the poor. The typical Christian faces many more routine demands on his or her charitable dollar than a secular graduate of Big State U.

One of Guelzo's complaints is that Christian schools are not selective enough. He proves his point by showing the high acceptance rate at many of the colleges. But a study of the percentage of students admitted at Union University, for example, would not tell the story Guelzo suggests it does. Union likely admits a majority of the students who apply, but that is part of its model. Union sets out to attract applications from students who are a good fit spiritually and academically, and it actively discourages the ones who are not a good fit. Union's selectivity would be better measured by a look at the mean ACT scores of its recent freshman classes, which have been very high. Other schools use a similar model. It is not necessary to turn down a lot of students if you can get good ones to apply.

Another problem is that Christian colleges lack the means to sponsor doctoral programs except for those in professional training areas, such as education or counseling, in which students can count on improving their income by getting the degree. Christian universities are typically unable to afford the graduate fellowships or stipends expected by budding scholars who do not foresee themselves getting rich teaching history or English. This is a significant missed opportunity because it means that Christians largely cede academic graduate training to secular institutions. Dwell on the cultural importance here. Christian colleges and universities, for the most part, *do not* produce professors in the traditional academic areas (arts, humanities, sciences, and social sciences). Professors in these areas are almost all trained at secular universities. Notre Dame and Baylor are the notable exceptions in that both are running traditional PhD programs with graduate teaching and research assistantships. Baylor's decision to move into that realm has been courageous, farsighted, and culturally important.

It is also the case that scholars at Christian institutions are at a competitive disadvantage when it comes to the pursuit of publication. At the large state schools, and in most elite private ones, professors teach only two courses each semester, sometimes fewer. Professors at Christian colleges usually teach four courses per semester, which is a consuming task if the professor does it well.

I could go on. Christian colleges have fewer scholarly centers and think tanks, hold fewer conferences, and publish fewer journals. We who are at Christian colleges are fighting hard to accomplish our missions, but scarcity is an everyday reality. We scrutinize our expenditures very carefully.

Professor Guelzo is right to point to problems. There are some. But he has also missed the ascendancy of some Christian universities in the sector under discussion. Baylor has already been discussed, but there are other bright spots. For example, just as one Christian school, Lambuth University, announced its closing in Jackson, Tennessee, Lambuth's longtime sister school, Union University, enjoyed record enrollments and was in the midst of a successful capital campaign to build a beautiful library on a campus that has been transformed during the last couple of decades. Union's budget has nearly quintupled over that period and the school outperforms just about all of its peers in terms of financial health.

The reality is that Christian universities, as a sector, are likely to undergo some serious sifting. One knowledgeable observer suggested to me that several will close in the next decade. I agree with Guelzo that there are very possibly too many and that we would benefit from consolidation. Imagine if Baylor stood as the research flagship and there were also five to ten very strong liberal arts universities. They would all be cultural game-changers if they remained faithful.

We do not control the life and death of universities, though, from some central Christian planning office for what we perceive to be the maximum advantage. The response of our colleges and universities to the creative destruction of a free society in the area of higher education will be planned in some cases, spontaneous in others, and providential all around.

There has begun to be talk of a higher education bubble. Certainly, tuition prices have increased at a rate substantially higher than inflation for many years. Those of us educated just a couple of decades ago experience sticker shock when we see the bills students face today. If the economic situation continues to be one of little or no growth, and government has to make spending cuts in order to deal with fiscal crises, the prospects for colleges and universities, which rely on private prosperity and government subsidies or financing, appear to be unpromising.

Add to these new realities the fact that technology is beginning to offer the potential to revolutionize education and we see the seeds of significant upheaval. Educational content is now everywhere. A person can learn nearly anything, anytime, anywhere on a bewildering array of devices. The Internet has graduated from a marginal existence as a frustrating and hard-to-reach resource to being in the air like some magical field for all to access.

When the universities began, a significant part of their appeal was their collections of books. In the age of massively democratizing trends with regard to information, a student no longer has to enter a university's grounds and buildings in order to find and read information. Having the information is not enough.

Institutions have protected themselves, to some degree, by gaining quasi-monopolistic powers over credentialing. They say who is and who is not college educated. The Christian colleges participate in that power. Employers buy into the system because it acts as a filter. They use higher education as a form of quality control on their applicants. Students buy in because there are not good ways to circumvent the system.

But institutions of higher education cannot simply count on credentialing power to sustain them. The forces of free-market creative destruction find ways over, around, and through. There was a time when many lawyers were self-educated. Such a time could come again. The same could be true of other fields. Individuals could educate themselves or make other arrangements for mentoring and training and then prove themselves through respected exams or simulation exercises. John Stuart Mill envisaged such a system back in the nineteenth century.

Another serious challenge is that education is in danger of becoming a commodity like heating oil, orange juice, copper, or soybeans. Retailers are cropping up to soak up as much demand (and federal and state dollars) for the commodity as they can. The Kaplan company, for example, recently made a big play to move from offering SAT preparation courses to forming its own university with satellite campuses around the country.

What all this means is that all colleges and universities must find ways to prove their value to the student if they are to continue to command a substantial portion of social resources. I think that the answer will include distinctiveness in terms of philosophy, critical thinking, character formation, and community.

To the extent that professors simply convey information, they will become obsolete. Substantively, instructors of this type already are. The credentialing power keeps them relevant for now. The best professors, though, will understand how to be sagacious mentors for young people. They will have a vision of teaching that goes beyond prepackaged, easily digestible textbook industry capsules and extends into the philosophy underlying a field or an activity. The great publisher Henry Luce, who founded the *Time-Life* empire, made an enormous success of *Sports Illustrated* (though he was not much of a fan of sports himself) because he knew it was important to do more than simply report on wins, losses, and statistics. He realized that one had to care about the philosophy of sport and the story of it. Philosophy, story, the why, the music—these are the things that represent the upper level of education.

Professors in every field will need to have the ability to function as guides. Anyone can get through a journey with a map (and there are a lot of maps out there online), but we know that if you want to get the most you can out of a trip (or a quest) then you need a guide, a person who is familiar with the terrain, is a good translator of the language, and has a profound understanding of the fundamentals. The best universities will hire those kinds of professors and will cultivate a living and learning community of instructors, staff, and students. This last part is difficult for the online players to duplicate. A great deal of learning occurs through community interaction around and outside the classroom, just as it does within it.

The new situation is both a potential threat and a boon to Christian colleges and universities. It is a great threat to the extent that these institutions simply try to participate as just another organization in the market offering a service that can be obtained from many other providers. If Christian schools go in that direction, they will suffer from an inability to compete on price with state universities and discount online retailers. They will also suffer a diminution of their mission because market imperatives will eventually overtake those of faith.

On the other hand, the new reality is a boon because it offers an opportunity to excel where Christian colleges *should* have an advantage. If the great mass of educational content is commoditized, then the college that is able to differentiate itself can make a compelling pitch to students and their families. Christian colleges can successfully argue that the best education connects with the mind, the body, and the soul.

Accordingly, when Christian institutions have done their job well, they will offer students the chance to work with professors who are trustworthy and insightful mentors who are ready and willing to lead students in a learning community. Christian colleges should be great citadels of educational integrity, trust, insight, and community excellence in the pursuit of truth about the world, its Creator, and humanity. In other words, if Christian colleges are committed to *being* Christian rather than simply acting as educational institutions with Christian ornamentation, they should have the wherewithal to survive and thrive in the changing environment.

Eleven

THE FUTURE
OF HIGHER EDUCATION

I t is a difficult thing to write about the future of one's own field of endeavor, especially if the forecast is for change. However, that is the forecast. Change is coming.

One thing is clear. Education at all levels will be transformed by the dominance of choice. Christians have often bemoaned the disintegration of a shared cultural consensus (specifically, a Christian cultural consensus), but much more than the edifice of a broad Christendom will be pulled down and reconstructed into something new. The large institutions of the twentieth century will face a continuing revolution of personalization and individual autonomy.

The America of the twentieth century scaled its institutions up in order to take advantage of economies of scale and to serve the needs of a rapidly growing population. Government agencies grew large and gained jurisdiction over the lives of large numbers of people. Congress provided a broad tuition benefit to the great masses of veterans that shifted a gigantic new demographic into colleges and universities. The mega-universities of today rose out of that paradigm shift. They were also stimulated by the powerful growth of the United States economy, which offered nearly endless opportunities to those willing to do things such as take on extra education. Public dollars flowed into higher education. Private dollars (specifically, tuition dollars) followed in their wake. After all, if a good is offered at less than its real cost, the rational consumer buys and buys and buys.

Over time, the combination of subsidies, growing consumer demand, and the introduction of the wired campus (necessitating lots of IT infrastructure and personnel) have worked together to substantially increase the costs involved in operating colleges and universities. In addition, the schools have waged a war of improvement in their facilities and programs in an effort to attract a larger share of students and the dollars associated with them. (Note how rare it is now for students to share bathrooms with everyone on their floor in a new dormitory. The older dorms were just a step above barracks. In some cases, they actually *were* rehabilitated barracks.) The result—which we have also seen in the highly subsidized field of health care—has been a rapid increase in the price of tuition and fees.

From Public Money to Private Money

Today, we have reached a point of decision about the universities. Will the public sector continue to pour money into the institutions? The answer appears to be no. Part of the reason for rising tuition at the state schools is that legislatures are providing fewer subsidies for tuition. Parents and students have to make up the difference. The federal outlook also looks bad. Entitlements such as Social Security and Medicare show little sign of loosening their grip on the federal budget. At the same time, defense spending is high. Interest on the national debt has the potential to explode, thus further inhibiting the government's ability to spend. Pell grants and loan guarantees may well be vulnerable when budget cutting ceases to be a debate and becomes a necessity. As public money declines as a proportionate influence on higher education, private money (real consumer dollars) will have a greater influence. Private money feels more distress at high prices than public money does. While higher education was perceived as a subsidized good available at less than the real cost, consumers could not get enough of it. But as real costs begin to be felt by the buyers, they want a greater guarantee of return on investment. They also want more options and flexibility. In other words, they are treating higher education as a market good rather than as some separate, hallowed social institution deserving deference and sacrifice on their part.

The Revolution in Distributing Educational Content

This greater demand on private money to pay for the good of higher education is occurring during a period of amazing technological innovation. We live in an era when it is possible to access almost any kind of content from almost anywhere. In America, for example, the great majority of us possess computing devices that we can use to read, listen to, watch, and talk about virtually any subject. These computing devices are outstanding vessels into which educational information can be poured. The book was already an extremely good technology. Consequently, the profusion of libraries and the growth of personal book collections made it possible to access information in a very democratic fashion. But the Internet has made it possible to augment that technology of text with pictures, sound, and links to far more information than could ever be contained in a single book. The new digital packages are up to the task of distributing information, and even some teaching, very efficiently.

The revolution in distributing educational content makes economies of scale available to colleges and universities. For example, a college could develop an extremely good online course in American government and offer it to as many students as would like to sign up. A class of that nature can be set up with multiple-choice exams that can be graded automatically. Such a course would be especially helpful to large state universities, which have struggled with the logistics of offering general courses to huge populations. No more need for giant auditoriums to host US History 101 at the big state schools. What was sometimes done awkwardly with communal videotape could be done efficiently with online distribution.

Larger Possible Changes Ahead

The really interesting twist here is that courses could simply be purchased by institutions. James Q. Wilson had one of the best-selling American government textbooks. I taught a class using his book recently. Prior to teaching that course, it had been some time since I had offered a standard American government section. To my amazement, the book brought with it something like a course in a box. It would have been possible to teach the course with very little work on my part. I had the book, PowerPoint slides for every chapter, prewritten exams, short instructor outlines, and other course materials. It is only one additional step for the publisher to include lectures by the great James Q. Wilson himself. Include that additional element and you have a fairly complete class taught by a master. The institution could then assign a graduate assistant or a cheap adjunct professor to meet with the class once a week for questions, conversation, clarification, and evaluation.

Though this road is attractive in many respects, it contains the seeds of woe for universities. An academic publisher such as Cengage or Pearson will eventually find a way to cut the middleman out of the equation entirely. Why could not the publisher find a way to get its comprehensive courses accredited and made available to students anywhere who wanted to take them and apply them as credit to a transcript? Such an eventuality is not too far away. In a sense, there are teachers and there are students. The relentless advance of creative destruction fueled by technology ruthlessly removes intermediaries. Universities could end up in the position of intermediaries unless they are very strategic in planning their next moves. We could see a day in which professors, rather than institutions, seek accreditation, while students put together official transcripts of courses taken from various accredited professors. Such an outcome is a real possibility.

But then again, what can be extrapolated is not always a good foundation for predicting the future. The first thing that can be said is that the traditional mode of university education is unlikely to simply disappear. The more likely outcome is that the number of options for obtaining an education are going to increase dramatically. Some schools will purposefully continue in the way we now take for granted. Others will host a blended experience of online or prepackaged content presented alongside classroom instruction. Pure online options will become more sophisticated and will have superior content. The pressure on everything to become better and cheaper will increase.

That will happen, but the effort of doing so will come at a cost for universities and for professors. For many years, schools have simply increased tuition incrementally and then used the additional income to fund new programs, pay raises, and other expenses. That era is over. It is officially time to innovate in ways that will give students greater value for less money. The institutions that fail to do that (except for those that have giant endowments) will see their competitive position erode consistently over time. Part of the adjustment will come by reforming the cost structures of universities. To give one simple example, professors will be less and less able to assume that tuition dollars can pay for them to travel to conferences and pay for time to write and do research. Those activities will continue, but they will bear a heavy weight of justification.

A Caste System for Professors

A deeper implication is that the profession of college teaching may develop a more stratified caste system than it currently has. We are all accustomed to the system of tenure-track jobs known as assistant professor, associate professor, and full professor. The ranks carry different pay levels and often delegate more grunt work of teaching downward. Each one of these professors represents a long-term investment. Professors are not lightly dropped. As a result, when schools have desired to cut expenses they have resorted to using alternative labor to achieve the same result in teaching. They hire adjunct professors who require no more than a single semester commitment and a small fee with no benefits. Many schools with extensive graduate programs employ graduate students to the same effect. This trend of more cheaply extending the professoriate will continue. Fewer and fewer tenure-track professors will be hired. Instead, schools will make increasing use of visiting professors, contract faculty, adjuncts, and individuals with master's degrees to facilitate some of the prefab courses. As a result, institutions will gain significant labor flexibility. Have a bad year recruiting students? You can just hire fewer seasonal instructors. The caste-like nature of the professoriate will be more obvious than ever as a relatively small number of professors enjoy full rank and privileges compared to those who round out the teaching force more economically. Ultimately, the professoriate will mainly be made up of those who are gifted at creating educational content or performing highly useful research. Everyone else will become more of an educational facilitator. Educational facilitators will provide value by answering questions, giving assignments, and evaluating students. Their ranks will grow substantially. The job will likely command less prestige and income than the old-style professoriate has come to enjoy as those perks will be available to a diminishing few. What is true of the traditional professor's position is simply the truth about virtually all professions as market forces push change and innovation. Fewer privileges will be protected. Proof of value added to the process will be an exacting test that more and more people will feel in their work.

Fighting to Stay in the Traditional Space

Just as the nature of college teaching will change, so will institutions. There will be less room in the market for traditional providers of college education as we have understood it. That model is not going away, but it will be the premium model. Those schools who wish to maintain a truly traditional presence will have to be ready to defend their position in that market. For some colleges, it will be easy. Some schools will be able to continue in the traditional space on the sheer power of accumulated wealth and tradition. Those who do not have those benefits (especially the wealth), such as many of the faithful Christian institutions, will only be able to stay in the traditional space to the extent that they are able to demonstrate a very clear difference in their offerings. They will need to show that residence on their campuses means something to students after four years both in terms of education and character formation. It once very clearly meant something to be a "Princeton man," for instance. If many of the evangelical schools want to persist in the premium, traditional market, there will need to be substance behind the idea of, for example, a Union or Wheaton man or woman. That substance will refer back to Christian orthodoxy, spiritual seriousness, sanctification, and fluency in Christian thinking.

But even in the institutions that do everything right to stay in the traditional space, the changes alluded to with regard to the professoriate are likely to occur. In addition, there will be continued pressure for the liberal arts and other portions of the core curriculum to justify themselves. Professional schools (and their accreditors) will press for more hours out of the whole. The likely result is continued diminution in the traditional core unless universities who value it are able to make a compelling case for its contribution. Appeals to being well-rounded or well-educated strike the marketplace with diminishing force when prices are perceived to be high. This problem is one of the most painful for me because it was only later in life that I discovered the liberal arts and their amazing value in forming judgment and perspective. Unless we find a way to counter this particular trend (perhaps through philanthropic subsidies of liberal arts offerings), the result is an inevitable coarsening of the culture (which, of course, we have seen) and a loss of the long view when evaluating many of the important decisions we must make as individuals or as communities.

The Most Vulnerable Sector

Contrary to expectations, the institutions that will come under the greatest pressure will ultimately not be the traditional schools (though they will have to grapple with change). The greatest pressure will apply to the entities currently believed to be the wave of the future, which are the online programs. If you are considering a long-term financial investment in the University of Phoenix or one of its competitors, I would urge you to go elsewhere with your funds. The online education companies are the closest thing to pure intermediaries in the whole higher education sector. If the producers of online educational content make the leap I have suggested they will make, then entire online courses of study will be available from big textbook publishers instead of from the University of Phoenix or Strayer or some other provider. In fact, even the publishers will eventually be vulnerable as teams of accomplished and entrepreneurial academics could put together their own courses, seek accreditation for them, and then offer them on the market directly to students. The key is a move from accreditation for institutions to accreditation for educational content, but it is a logical and efficient move that will satisfy needs in the market. Contrary to conventional wisdom, the pure or mostly online institutions have far less to protect them from creative destruction in the educational market than do the more traditional entities. Traditional colleges and universities are able to offer a full-orbed experience, which insulates them at least somewhat from the market pressures that hit commodities hardest. The University of Phoenix is much more of a commodity player.

Projecting Still Further Out

The most important part of the argument so far is that educational content creators will work to cut intermediaries out of the equation. Publishers will struggle to survive. Commodity institutions will be cut out. Traditional colleges and universities will resist being cut out for a few reasons. First, they are able to provide the college experience that Americans still value and hope to provide for their children. Second, they often have distinctive character and customs that appeal to parents and students. Third, they can offer physical community and the relationships that follow from those. Fourth, in some cases they have made infrastructure investments that are not easily replicated. For example, I think of Union University's nursing simulation labs. They are costly and offer education that is not easily provided elsewhere. Just to reiterate, though, despite the buffers, traditional players will have to be able to make a convincing sales pitch for the value of their degrees. They will also have to contain or cut costs vigorously in the near future.

As we look further out into the future, we find the question of the relationship of the professor to institutions. If creative destruction has a tendency to cause disintermediation, what will happen to the relationship between professors and the institutions to which they have typically been tied? To the extent that infrastructure, machinery, and specialized materials are needed, then professors and institutions will still be tied together. But what about the many college courses in which what mainly occurs is a transfer of information and expertise between the professor and the student? Will we eventually see a situation in which college professors become independently accredited in the same way lawyers and doctors are? Will it be possible someday for students to create their own patchwork transcript of work taken from a variety of independent professors, institutes, think tanks, hospitals, government agencies, corporations, and universities? Given the conditions of high price, rapid technological innovation, disintermediation, and great market scrutiny of the value proposition, I think such a general turn is possible.

If professors do gain a degree of independence from institutions, it seems likely that alliances between the two will remain. In many cases, professors will sell their classes to institutions that will then add educational facilitators to the mix to provide the student with more assistance. Universities will also be able to provide professors with a baseline income they may need to provide the basis for their more entrepreneurial activities. They may make arrangements to pay professors less and with more flexible terms, which will ensure an affiliation and at least some dedicated time from the professor for the specific school. What is almost certain to end is tenure as we know it. The security of tenure fits poorly with the dynamism and flexibility of a modern and constantly evolving economy. Professors and colleges will form alliances, but on much more fluid terms than before. In many cases, the relationship may be based on spiritual and ideological relationships as much or more than economic ones.

Conclusion

Predicting the future is notoriously difficult. Even physical scientists find it difficult, as evidenced by the magazine covers of the 1970s that promised a new ice age, which now stand in stark contrast to the dire predictions of global warming that dominated the last decade.

But I think the broad outlines of what I have discussed here will hold. Traditional institutions that really have a tradition and distinctiveness will survive, although in smaller numbers than today. This is good news for institutions like Union University that are serious about their mission and identity. Institutions that are purely online will suffer massive competition from the creators of educational content. Schools will make greater use of professor extenders very much like health care institutions rely on physician extenders. The concept of accreditation will expand to professors and to courses rather than residing simply with colleges. The relationship between professors and institutions will become much more flexible. Some of these changes will occur in the near term. Others may take decades to reach fruition.

One thing is certain, though. Higher education is directly in the path of creative destruction. The smart players will figure out the right market to serve and how to offer the best value for the lowest price to their customers. All the players in the game need to be figuring out where they sit on the game board and what their right path forward is.

Twelve

CHRISTIAN SCHOOLS
AND RACIAL REALITIES

I live in Jackson, Tennessee. Our town of about one hundred thousand people sits between Memphis and Nashville. One of the
outstanding features of Jackson is that it plays host to an unusually
large number of Christian and other private schools. Three public-
school sized parochial (or semiparochial in one case) entities occupy
positions on the north side of town. Another smaller one with a great
books emphasis (the paradoxically new thing in evangelical Christian
education) is the proud owner of a smaller building that had been
outgrown by one of the three flagship schools. It also happens that
the public schools of Jackson only recently gained their independence from federal supervision dating back to the racial tensions of
segregation and desegregation.

Many view Christian schools with suspicion because a significant
number of them began operation in the period when the United States
was grappling most earnestly with desegregating American school
systems in the hopes of vindicating our fundamental belief in equal
opportunity. Statistics buttress this suspicion. From 1961 to 1971,
enrollment in non-Catholic private schools doubled. The natural
inference is that enthusiasm for Christian schooling was little more

than a cover for racism. Some even referred to emerging Christian schools as "new segregation academies."[1]

My argument is that while we observe clear covariation between desegregation and the rise of non-Catholic private schooling, it is also the case that other explanatory factors are available to explain at least part of the rise. My further contention is that even if we can vitiate the racial concern to some degree, there is a continuing moral and spiritual burden, which remains to be adequately addressed.

I met with a professor in my university's school of education to discuss the issue. Ben Phillips has a unique pedigree in that he has previously served as a principal of a large and racially balanced public school in the Memphis metro area and then later in the same capacity at a largely white Christian school here in Jackson. I asked him about the inference of racism. He conceded that the inference is a natural one, but disputed the assumption that parents necessarily fled the public schools for invidious reasons. While admitting throughout our conversation that race was then and possibly is now one of many potential motivators, he said, "It is important to remember that school desegregation and busing efforts represented an unprecedented and large disruption and intrusion upon established routines for parents, families, and schools." Even though the end goals of desegregation were honorable and necessary, one might not be surprised to find members of local communities scrambling to avoid government moves that they found unpredictable and burdensome for children as well as for adults.

Another important feature of the question at hand is the cultural change that was occurring at the time. The 1960s and 1970s were the period in which issues of religion and worldview became much more salient in public education.

Perhaps the single most emblematic illustration of cultural change was the Supreme Court's 1962 decision in *Engel v. Vitale* to end officially sanctioned prayer in public schools. The court followed that case closely with its 1963 decision in *Abington v. Schempp* to block official Bible readings. Taken together, the two cases repre-

---

1. Virginia Davis Nordin and William Lloyd Turner took note of this view in their article "More than Segregation Academies: The Growing Protestant Fundamentalist Schools," *The Phi Delta Kappan* 61, no. 6 (1980): 391–94.

sented a firm disestablishment of Christianity (especially Protestant Christianity) from the public school system. Even today, the public claim that secular liberals "threw God out of the schools" draws forth an appreciative response from many Americans.

In addition, sex education in the schools became a major controversy. Large numbers of parents viewed the incorporation of sex education into the curriculum as a replacement for the teaching of parents and churches. The reaction of parents to protest or flee sex education is often pilloried as a form of repressive hysteria, but they may have been justified. As Thomas Sowell has pointed out in *The Vision of the Anointed*, the percentage of fifteen- to nineteen-year-old girls who had "engaged in sex was higher at every age from 15 through 19 by 1976 than it was just five years earlier." Sowell also noted that "the rate of teenage gonorrhea tripled between 1956 and 1975."[2] One might add explosions in both the abortion rate and teen pregnancy during the relevant period to the roll call. The issue has staying power. Many parents (especially Christian ones) wish to preserve the more traditional view of sexuality and resent the idea that a taxpayer-funded representative of the state might teach their child differently.

Changes such as those considered above added to smoldering resentments over the teaching of evolution, which picked up more steam in the late 1950s as some argued that the Soviet success with *Sputnik* meant that American science education was unsatisfactory. A lack of teaching on evolution was one of the exhibits to which reformers pointed, which led to renewed efforts to push states to be more vigorous in their coverage of the topic in schools. That issue continues to be litigated in courts even very recently (*Kitzmiller v. Dover Area School District* [2005]) with both sides attaching huge symbolic importance to the outcome, which is easy to understand as many atheists begin their testimonies of unbelief with vignettes centered on hearing about the theory of evolution for the first time. Those testimonies represent stories of liberation that atheists wish to be repeated, and such testimonies represent reviews of falls from grace for Christians.

---

2. Thomas Sowell, *The Vision of the Anointed: Self-Congratulation as a Basis for Social Policy* (New York: Basic Books, 1995), 18.

These cultural developments—apart from the civil rights movement—helped push many Christian parents to choose private education just as the heavy Protestant influence in public schools in years prior had helped drive the explosive growth of Catholic schooling. Catholics had resisted the broadly Protestant establishment in the public schools by setting up their own schools. Now, conservative Protestants were doing the same thing as they found their own welcome had become worn. If they wanted an education for their children that would reinforce their beliefs, they would need to start new schools.[3] And they did so. The movement has picked up steam as Christians have added whole new layers of classical schools and homeschooling.

Being able to provide reasonably good answers for why Christian schools began to pop up in larger numbers during the period of desegregation can blunt the impact of accusations of racism, but it does not necessarily help with the issue of effects. Part of the reason why racial wounds have failed to completely heal since the advent of *de jure* equality is that as soon as the doors opened to everyone, a sizeable number of folks began to make alternative arrangements. The blame can be spread around. Judges and policymakers sometimes chose tactics (such as forcing children to endure long bus rides to unfamiliar parts of their cities at early and late hours) to achieve integration that would have given even the most level-headed and fair-minded parent fits. There was also the problem that solutions had to be lived out by children rather than parents. For example, a parent might have had great thoughts about putting his or her white child into the minority at a largely black school, but the courage would not have been all that worthy of credit when the fact was that *the child* would be the one who experienced minority status. It is one thing to be Jackie Robinson. It is another to expect one's child to be the trailblazer. Finally, we might add that secular liberals probably unwittingly undermined the project of integration by overthrowing the slender Protestant establishment of faith and worldview in the schools during the critical span of years when integration efforts were ongoing. Still, all the good and valid explanations we might

---

3. Other authors have reached similar conclusions buttressed by empirical data. See Nordin and Turner, "More than Segregation Academies," 391–94.

adduce do not erase the damage that has been done and continues to accrue in ways known and unknown.

The toll has taken two forms. First, there is the sense of rejection African Americans have felt as whites fled hard-won integration. Second, there has been a problem in schools similar to the trouble of the housing projects. Whenever institutions concentrate disproportionate numbers of individuals in one place whose lives have been marked by unwed parents, poor employment records, crime, a lack of role models, and negative social fashions (such as the idea that studying is a "white" behavior), the prospect for social improvement and vertical mobility declines. There can be little question that trends toward suburbanization, private schooling, and homeschooling remove many children who come from homes with more cultural capital from the schools where they might add helpful values, attitudes, and habits to the community of students. And, of course, the parents of those children are likewise not present to help share tasks of volunteering and leadership.

All of this leaves the Christian schooling project in something of a quandary. On the one hand, Christians have a strong mandate to help the disadvantaged. Being in the public schools is one way to do that. On the other hand, many have worked hard (and made heavy sacrifices in terms of time and money) to build institutions offering an education for mind, body, and soul, which they believe in strongly as a foundation for their children. Though the logic of something like faithful presence (to use James Davison Hunter's term) in the schools has a great deal to say for it, there is something not quite right about an appeal to the folks in the Christian school movement to the effect that they should fold their tents.

Ben Phillips explained to me that when he was the principal of a strong Christian school following his years in Memphis, "I wanted more minority students. I think a big part of the problem is that they were closed out by price." So far, the response of conservative Christians has been to advocate for taxpayer-funded tuition vouchers. That project, however, has been fraught with difficulty both because of perceived church-state issues (a modest *legal* problem) and the resistance of public school supporters, who are worried about budgets already, to allow any resources to go to the private school system that they perceive, correctly, to stand in judgment of their own efforts (a much bigger *political* problem).

Assuming a continuing deadlock over the issue of school choice, the best answer may be for conservative Christians to find other ways to create greater access to their institutions for those from whom they are suspected of fleeing. It is a burden of history not easily shrugged off, even by generations who did not make the world in which they live. We inherit debts other than the kind governments incur on their balance sheets. But the racial unification of the American church might best begin in the Christian schoolhouse before it takes hold in the Sunday services. It is a home mission (as the Baptists might call it) awaiting a champion and a movement.

Conclusion

POLITICAL THOUGHTS
ON THE RESURRECTION

And on the pedestal these words appear:
"My name is Ozymandias, king of kings:
Look on my works, ye Mighty, and despair!"
Nothing beside remains. Round the decay
Of that colossal wreck, boundless and bare
The lone and level sands stretch far away.

—Shelley, "Ozymandias"

When I think about why I am a Christian, I reflect on the almost completely silent priest-psychiatrist character in Walker Percy's novel *Lancelot*. Over several sessions, he has listened to the sometimes mad, sometimes lucid and insightful, spoken thoughts of an apparent lunatic with whom he has some history. The half-crazed Lancelot has concluded that the existence of swinishness, indecency, and evil in the world demands harshness in return. Lancelot, the man who discovered that evil really exists, plans to be the first man, hopefully among many, who will not tolerate the grossness, ugliness, and lack of honor in the world any longer. He will act. It will be a harsh thing when he does. Indeed, he already has reacted murderously to what he has seen.

At the end of his tale, he notices that his priest-psychiatrist friend, who has listened patiently while never quite looking at him, is now facing him directly. It turns out that he is ready to speak. We know that the priest has been in doubt about his own faith. What he has heard has caused him to consider his own beliefs and what course of action he might take. Shortly before being discharged, mad Lancelot asks the quiet priest who has listened so patiently, "Is there anything you wish to tell me before I leave?" In answer, the priest simply says, "Yes." It is the only word he speaks.[1] This yes is the last of a series of affirmations, but this one holds a gigantic meaning waiting to be expressed. It has been disclosed in the narrative that he is leaving the priest-psychiatrist business to shepherd a small rural parish. We understand that the trajectory of his life has changed. He is about to say why it has changed. He is about to tell Lancelot what is wrong with his plan to become an avenging angel in the place of a God he assumes is either nonexistent or has abandoned the field. When I read the book, that yes made the hair on the back of my neck stand up and made me shiver. What universe is contained in that yes?

As I reflect on the question, I realize that I do not know all of the things that he will say. But I think it is almost a certainty that part of the answer is the same as what Paul said to the men of Athens in the Areopagus. Consider for a moment Acts 17:30–31:

> Therefore having overlooked the times of ignorance, God is now declaring to men that all *people* everywhere should repent, because He has fixed a day in which He will judge the world in righteousness through a Man whom He has appointed, *having furnished proof to all men by raising Him from the dead* [italics added].

Paul confronts the men of that ancient debating society with the New Testament's astounding message. Jesus claimed to be the Son of God, the way, the truth, and the life. The question is, is it true? Paul answers that in an unphilosophical, blunt way. He says something like this: "God raised Jesus from the dead. And this is proof

---

1. Walker Percy, *Lancelot* (New York: Ivy Books, 1977), 241.

that what I have said is true. This is why I can give you a real God to replace your unknown one."

The Modern Settlement

If you find that you accept Paul's claim, then your entire life will change. You have discovered your true master, the one who exceeds all the false ones found scattered all over the world. The matter of true and false masters interests me. I am a political thinker. I dwell often on what the resurrection means for law and government. At a minimum, I think that it is here that we have the seeds of a rejection of the modern settlement of the question of politics and religion.

The Christian faith is not just a religion like any other religion. You are not expected to simply accept the word of some enlightened soul. Religions are not all the same. They do not all say the same thing. They do not all have the same likelihood of being true.

You should not be a Christian because you feel it works for you or because you like the message aesthetically the way you like a song or a postcard. You should not be a Christian because it is what your family believes or because it is part of your culture. If those things are the basis for faith, then we should absolutely accept the modern settlement, because then it is the case that we are not so much interested in knowing the truth as we are in just filling some need. Harmony is a need we have, too. And if there is no truth, then we should privilege harmony. But what if there is truth? Do we have a hope of knowing it?

You should be a Christian because in seeking the truth about this world, who we are, and what happens after we die, you have concluded with the millions that there is a legitimate hope for humankind in the person of Jesus Christ. It is a legitimate hope rooted in the stuff of time and space and history.

Let us follow closely upon that thought. Look at what Paul writes in 1 Corinthians 15:3–8:

> For I delivered to you as of first importance what I also received, that Christ died for our sins according to the Scriptures, and that He was buried, and that He was raised on the third day according to the Scriptures, and that He appeared to Cephas, then to the twelve. After that He appeared to more than five

hundred brethren at one time, most of whom remain until now, but some have fallen asleep; then He appeared to James, then to all the apostles; and last of all, as to one untimely born, He appeared to me also.

The Christian church is built on the resurrection as a public claim of fact. In this passage, Paul is saying, in effect, "Look, there were over five hundred witnesses. Some of them are dead now, but many are still alive. Ask them."

Christianity offers something unusual in the area of religion. Instead of relying on some Gnostic secret knowledge ("No one can be told what the Matrix is …"), the Christian faith began as a falsifiable proposition (which was never falsified). The early church claimed the resurrection as evidence, and the church was not defeated, though many would have sought to defeat it if they had the ammunition.

The existence of evidence is not always conclusive, but it changes the playing field in important ways. Christianity is not purely about revelation. Gary Habermas, a faithful Christian who has spent his career studying the resurrection, has argued that even if you do not accept the inspired nature of the New Testament, you still have to grapple with the historic claim of the church that Christ rose from the dead. And people do grapple with it. This is why explanations like the swoon theory developed, which holds that Christ was seen again because the crucifixion failed to kill him. Advocates of the swoon theory do not believe the Scriptures are inspired, but they do feel the need to address the claim that Jesus was seen after he was supposed to be moldering in the crypt.

The underlying point is that the substance of Christianity can be considered to some degree through the exercise of one's reason. Christianity has a real world *either/or*. Either Christ really rose from the dead, or we follow him in vain.

My colleague Scott Huelin once suggested to me that the resurrection of Christ collapses the distance between reason and revelation. This is related to another political point. Legal and political theorists sometimes argue that religious rhetoric is always inappropriate to political discourse. They would say it is not only impolite, but unvirtuous to make religious points on a public issue, or maybe even to make secular points motivated by religious thoughts or feelings.

If Christianity is not purely about revelation, but is also related to reason, the critique does not stand up quite so well. It is not, as these thinkers would charge, necessarily inaccessible to those outside the church.

Resurrection and Death

Death is an important issue in political theory. For example, the difference in the apprehension of death between Hobbes and Locke affects their respective philosophies.

Today, we are differently situated relative to death than virtually everyone who lived on the face of the earth prior to the last one hundred years. The generations prior to our more recent vintage had a much greater familiarity with death. It was common to have lost a sibling, a child, a spouse, a friend. The realization that an infection or an illness could easily prove fatal was simply a matter of being practical.

Our situation appears to be different. Thanks to the availability of anesthesia and antibiotics, we have developed the expectation that we will live to an old age. Death is unlikely to claim us ahead of our time. We may feel we have tamed death and segregated it to a period of life when it is far away and can be safely ignored.

One possible consequence for political theory is that we avoid questions of the good life for the individual and the community in favor of visions of autonomy and atomism. I began thinking about this trend when reading Tolstoy's tale of Ivan Ilyich. Ilyich is a man who has achieved social position and professional prestige. Ridiculously, he injures himself attempting to hang curtains and suffers some kind of internal disorder that kills him slowly over a period of many weeks. He tries to take satisfaction in his social and professional achievements, but finds himself unable to gain any peace until he considers more deeply the question of how he should have lived and what he might have done differently. Death provides perspective, but we think we are far from it.

Of course, our feeling of detachment from death is based on an illusion. In *Christ the Tiger*, Thomas Howard wrote:

When death is upon us, we slobber and cry out to heaven. But what is the real difference between being in a great transoceanic jet hurtling in flames toward the sea beneath, and being a few tenuous years from the same issue? In the one situation you know that you have perhaps two minutes of consciousness and identity left to you before you are blown across into nothingness. In the other you suppose, quite fondly, that you have a longer interval before the plunge. Our faculty for finding solace in this interval is a curious one. Apparently the cabins of airliners heading for the earth are scenes of wild shrieking and hysteria. What about? Death? But a minute before, as the travelers read their French phrase booklets and menus, or broke open their cardboard containers of salt, did they suppose they weren't going to die? What mythology enabled them to stay calm? Is there some definitive difference between death now and later?[2]

A couple of pages later:

We are all sitting on Death Row. One fine day the man comes, and we excuse ourselves awkwardly and disappear.[3]

These passages are dark, but you may suspect, of course, that the talk of Christ is coming. It is he who teaches us about "a kind of life that participates in the indestructible."[4] And it is he who demonstrated his victory over death in such a way as to give us reason to trust him.

Resurrection and Nationalism

My colleague Greg Ryan has twice lived in China for extended periods. I asked him if he had taken the opportunity to go to church while in China. He said he had gone on occasion to the Protestant churches licensed by the state. I told him I assumed that they were limited in some ways by the Chinese government and suggested that perhaps they were not permitted to criticize the regime. He said that was

---

2. Thomas Howard, *Christ the Tiger: A Postscript to Dogma* (Philadelphia: Lippincott, 1967), 136.

3. Howard, *Christ the Tiger*, 138.

4. Howard, *Christ the Tiger*, 154.

true. He then added spontaneously, "They don't much want them to talk about the resurrection either."

Now, why might the Chinese government want to avoid emphasis on the resurrection of Christ? The answer is that the resurrection is a repellent historical assertion to nationalists and totalizers who demand ultimate allegiance. Richard Niebuhr once wrote,

> The Christ who will not worship Satan to gain the world's kingdoms is followed by Christians who will worship only Christ in unity with the Lord whom he serves. And this is intolerable to all defenders of society who are content that many gods should be worshipped if only Democracy or America or Germany or the Empire receives its due, religious homage.... The implied charge against Christian faith is like the ancient one: it imperils society by its attack on its religious life; it deprives social institutions of their cultic, sacred character; by its refusal to condone the pious superstitions of tolerant polytheism it threatens social unity. The charge lies not only against Christian organizations which use coercive means against what they define as false religions, but against the faith itself.[5]

Christ takes precedence over whatever the program of the state is. True Christianity is a natural and avowed opponent of the Durkheimian social religion in which we worship our collective selves.

Rodney Stark has written, "The corollary that because God loves humanity, Christians may not please God unless they love one another was something entirely new."[6] This is a vision that goes beyond family, tribe, and nation. If Jesus is Lord, then the state must not be allowed to create ethnic or nationalistic hatreds of other human beings.

Reading Eric Metaxas' book about Dietrich Bonhoeffer, one spots the tragedy of the mistake that so many people made in their embrace of German Christianity during the Nazi era. They prioritized the Reich over Christ and the church, with devastating results. Bonhoeffer kept his priorities in their correct order. And, of course,

---

5. H. Richard Niebuhr, *Christ and Culture* (New York: Harper, 1956), 8–9.

6. Rodney Stark, *The Rise of Christianity* (San Francisco: HarperSanFrancisco, 1996), 212.

he was executed by the state. But he trusted in a resurrected Lord instead of a temporal Führer.

Toward the end of his massive study of the resurrection, *The Resurrection of the Son of God*, N. T. Wright includes a section titled "Resurrection and World Leadership." He notes that early Christians used the phrase "Son of God" to describe Jesus both knowing that pagan emperors had applied it to themselves and intending to confront them with "the world's true Lord." Calling Jesus the Son of God, in this sense, demonstrated the determination of early Christians to prevent themselves from being understood as "a private cult, a sect, a mystery religion." What began as an absurd challenge toward Rome launched by "a tiny group of nobodies" became so serious that within a couple of generations the might of Rome was trying, and failing, to stamp it out. According to Wright, what makes the resurrection so powerful is that it was a physical triumph over death. Christ did not merely die and go to heaven. This is critical. Wright says, "Death is the ultimate weapon of the tyrant; resurrection does not make a covenant with death, it overthrows it."[7]

Thus, the resurrection helps to provide proper perspective for the state. Jacques Maritain, the French Catholic scholar who played a significant role in the writing of the United Nations Declaration on Human Rights, properly explained that "the State is not a kind of collective superman; the State is but an agency entitled to use power and coercion, and made up of experts or specialists in public order and welfare, an instrument in the service of man. Putting man at the service of that instrument is political perversion."[8] In short, the state is made for man, not man for the state. People have souls and eternal destinies. States do not. Their works are mighty in their time, but like the claimed triumphs of Ozymandias, the self-anointed king of kings, they do not endure.

---

7. N. T. Wright, *The Resurrection of the Son of God* (Minneapolis: Fortress, 2003), 729–31.

8. Jacques Maritain, *Man and the State* (Washington, DC: Catholic University of America Press, 1998), 13.

INDEX OF NAMES

Index of Names

Made in the USA
Middletown, DE
05 June 2015